A BOOK OF DELIGHTS

An Anthology of Words and Pictures

A BOOK
OF DELIGHTS

AN ANTHOLOGY

OF WORDS AND PICTURES

CHOSEN AND ARRANGED BY

JOHN HADFIELD

LONDON : HAMISH HAMILTON

FIRST EDITION PUBLISHED 1954
REPRINTED 1954, 1955, 1956, 1957
THIS REVISED EDITION PUBLISHED 1977
BY HAMISH HAMILTON LTD
90 GREAT RUSSELL STREET LONDON WC1B 3PT

ISBN 241 89727 0

© JOHN CHARLES HEYWOOD HADFIELD 1954, 1977
DESIGNED BY JOHN HADFIELD AND JOHN LEWIS
PRINTED IN GREAT BRITAIN BY W. S. COWELL LTD
IPSWICH

THE PAINTING REPRODUCED ON THE HALF-TITLE
PAGE IS A DETAIL FROM CRIVELLI'S 'ANNUNCIATION'
THE FRONTISPIECE IS FROM A PAINTING BY GEORGE KNAPTON

INTRODUCTION

The world is so full of a number of things,
I'm sure we should all be as happy as kings.

WHEN I WAS A CHILD I was impressed, like many other children, but also a little puzzled, by Stevenson's familiar lines. I was puzzled by them only because happiness then seemed to me something unpredictable, not biddable at the command of an 'ought' or a 'should'. Today, though I have not sunk so deep in pessimism as Dr Johnson's conclusion that 'the natural flights of the human mind are not from pleasure to pleasure, but from hope to hope', I realize that happiness has often to be sought. That it can be found by looking, and can be cultivated by those who know how, is the conviction in which I have compiled this anthology.

Another of Dr Johnson's sayings was that 'our brightest blazes of gladness are commonly kindled by unexpected sparks'. But it would seem to me a surrender to fatalism, a shameful denial of free will, to assume that we cannot, whatever our limitations or circumstances, kindle some warmth of delight from fires which we light ourselves.

Such warmth, I hope, will at least glow and glimmer from the words and pictures and music which I have brought together in this book. If there is a constant theme—and it is either a very bold or a very dull anthologist who dares to claim that he has *always* kept to the point—it is the *accessibility* of delight, the belief that the greatest happiness can be found in the most common of experiences.

'Man', wrote Hazlitt, 'is the only animal that laughs and weeps; for he is the only animal that is struck with the difference between what things are and what they ought to be.' This book is not

v

intended as a denial of the existence of pain, sickness, grief, or even the apparently unaccountable state of melancholy. But it seeks no compromise with the quite indefensible state of *boredom*. I recognize no valid reason for being bored. At any moment, in almost any circumstances not completely governed by pain or grief, it should be possible to see, hear, feel or conjure up in the mind some revelation of delight. That one often fails to do so is a reflection either upon the alertness of one's senses or upon the slothfulness of one's mind.

In the pages which follow I have tried to illustrate, in the context of such common experiences as awakening, growing up, looking and listening, eating and drinking, loving, dreaming, making (in the sense of *creating*), understanding (in the widest sense of *worshipping*), and falling asleep, the ever-presence of delight, the immanence of happiness. I have also tried to represent, in a series of contrasted passages and pictures, the complementary states of 'being' and 'doing', into which almost all human experience can be divided.

'The race of delight is short', wrote Sir Thomas Browne, 'and pleasures have mutable faces.' The pleasures which show their faces in this book tend, I realize, to be reflective, unspectacular, and solitary. Quite a different book could be built round the delights of activity and society, on which I have only touched lightly. This, however, is one man's choice of delights, an even more personal commonplace book than my *Book of Beauty*. The fact that the original edition, which has been out of print for five years, went into a ninth impression suggests that a good many other people share my tastes.

In this revised edition I have retained the same framework and much of the content of the original; but I have incorporated some seventy fresh passages of verse and prose, and replaced ten of the colour plates with images that now appeal to me more.

1977   J.H.

ACKNOWLEDGEMENTS

THE COMPILER makes grateful acknowledgement of the facilities afforded by the private collectors and trustees of art galleries and museums named in the List of Illustrations.

For permission to reprint copyright passages of prose and verse acknowledgement is made to Jonathan Cape, The Hogarth Press and the executors of the Estate of C. Day-Lewis for a poem from C. Day-Lewis's *Collected Poems*, 1954; to Chatto & Windus and Doubleday & Company for a passage from *The Young Visiters* by Daisy Ashford; to Chatto & Windus and Harcourt Brace Jovanovitch for a passage from *A Rabbit in the Air* by David Garnett; to Constable & Company for passages from *Small Talk* by Sir Harold Nicolson, *Trivia* and *More Trivia* by Logan Pearsall Smith, and *Soliloquies in England* by George Santayana; to Constable & Company and Alfred A. Knopf for two poems from 170 *Chinese Poems* translated by Arthur Waley, copyright 1919, renewed 1947 by Arthur Waley; to J. M. Dent & Sons and Little, Brown & Company for a poem from Ogden Nash's *Good Intentions*, copyright 1940 by Ogden Nash; to J. M. Dent & Sons and New Directions Publishing Corporation, New York, for a poem from *The Poems of Dylan Thomas*, copyright 1946 by New Directions Publishing Corporation; to J. M. Dent & Sons and Zephyrus Press for a passage from *Ten Years Under the Earth* by Norbert Casteret; to J. M. Dent & Sons and E. P. Dutton & Company for a passage from *Coming Down the Seine* by Robert Gibbings; to Gerald Duckworth & Company for a poem from Harold Monro's *Collected Poems*, edited by Alida Monro, 1970; to Faber & Faber for a poem from *Collected Poems* by Michael Roberts; to the author and Hamish Hamilton for a poem from *Collected Poems*, copyright 1956, by Kathleen Raine; to William Heinemann, Laurence Pollinger, the Estate of the late Frieda Lawrence, and The Viking Press for a poem from D. H. Lawrence's *Pansies* and for a passage from Aldous Huxley's Introduction to *The Letters of D. H. Lawrence*; to the Hogarth Press and Harcourt Brace Jovanovitch for a passage from *A Room of One's Own* by Virginia Woolf; to Mr Laurie Lee for his poem, 'April Rise'; to the Longmans Group for a passage from *Chemistry in the Service of Man* by Alexander Findlay; to the Reverend K. S. P. McDowall for a passage from E. F. Benson's *As We Were*; to Methuen & Company for a poem from *Collected Poems* by Geoffrey Winthrop Young; to John Murray and Houghton Mifflin Company for a poem from Sir John Betjeman's *Collected Poems*; to Mrs Newton-Wood and the Oxford University Press for two poems by W. J. Turner; to A. D. Peters & Company for three poems by Gerald Bullett; to Mr G. T. Sassoon and the Viking Press for a poem by Siegfried Sassoon; to the Society of Authors as the literary representative of the Estate of James Stephens for a poem from *The Hill of Vision* by James Stephens; to The Society of Authors and Holt, Rinehart & Winston for two poems and passages of prose by Walter de la Mare; to Mr Raglan Squire for a poem by Sir John Squire; to A. P. Watt & Son, Dodd Mead & Company, and Miss D. E. Collins for a poem from *The Collected Poems of G. K. Chesterton*, copyright 1932 by Dodd Mead & Company, copyright renewed 1959 by Oliver Chesterton; to A. P. Watt and Lady Herbert for lines from *Derby Day* by A. P. Herbert.

Acknowledgement is also made for the music and words of 'I will give my love an apple', collected and arranged by Cecil Sharp and Ralph Vaughan Williams, to Novello & Company; and for the music of the first verse of 'Sleep' by Peter Warlock to the Oxford University Press, who also gave permission for the final bar to be altered for this volume. The compiler is much indebted to Mr Frank Waters for his assistance in the choice of songs and for his setting of the air for the song from *The Beggars' Opera*.

CONTENTS

NOTE. *The reference at the end of each passage is, in almost every instance, to the date and place of its first appearance in book form. The spelling and punctuation of the text has been modernized throughout. In order to allow as much room as possible for the illustrations, notes on their sources are printed at the end of the book.*

'LIFE,' said a gaunt widow, with a reputation for being clever,—
'life is a perpetual toothache'.

In this vein the conversation went on: the familiar topics were discussed of labour troubles, epidemics, cancer, tuberculosis, and taxation.

Next me there sat a little old lady who was placidly drinking her tea, and taking no part in the melancholy chorus. 'Well, I must say,' she remarked, turning to me and speaking in an undertone, 'I must say I enjoy life.'

'So do I,' I whispered.

'When I enjoy things,' she went on, 'I know it. Eating, for instance, the sunshine, my hot-water bottle at night. Other people are always thinking of unpleasant things. It makes a difference', she added, as she got up to go with the others.

'All the difference in the world,' I answered.

LOGAN PEARSALL SMITH
More Trivia, 1922

I: AWAKENING

DAY!
Faster and more fast,
O'er night's brim, day boils at last;
Boils, pure gold, o'er the cloud-cup's brim
Where spurting and suppressed it lay,
For not a froth-flake touched the rim
Of yonder gap in the solid gray
Of the eastern cloud, an hour away;
But forth one wavelet, then another, curled,
Till the whole sunrise, not to be suppressed,
Rose, reddened, and its seething breast
Flickered in bounds, grew gold, then overflowed the world.

ROBERT BROWNING, from 'Pippa Passes'
Bells and Pomegranates, 1841

So have I seen the sun kiss the frozen earth which was bound up
with the images of death and the colder breath of the North; and
then the waters break from their enclosures, and melt with joy, and
run in useful channels; and the flies do rise again from their little
graves in walls and dance a while in the air, to tell that there is joy
within and that the great mother of creatures will open the stock of
her new refreshment, become useful to mankind, and sing praises to
her Redeemer.

JEREMY TAYLOR
Twenty-five Sermons, 1653

A NEW DAY

SLOW bleak awakening from the morning dream
Brings me in contact with the sudden day.
I am alive—this I.
I let my fingers move along my body.
Realization warns them, and my nerves
Prepare their rapid messages and signals.
While Memory begins recording, coding,
Repeating; all the time Imagination
Mutters; You'll only die.

Here's a new day. O Pendulum move slowly!
My usual clothes are waiting on their peg.
I am alive—this I.
And in a moment Habit, like a crane,
Will bow its neck and dip its pulleyed cable,
Gathering me, my body, and our garment,
And swing me forth, oblivious of my question,
Into the daylight—why?

I think of all the others who awaken,
And wonder if they go to meet the morning
More valiantly than I;
Nor asking of this Day they will be living:
What have I done that I should be alive?
O, can I not forget that I am living?
How shall I reconcile the two conditions:
Living, and yet—to die?

Between the curtains the autumnal sunlight
With lean and yellow finger points me out;
The clock moans: Why? Why? Why?
But suddenly, as if without a reason,
Heart, Brain and Body, and Imagination
All gather in tumultuous joy together,
Running like children down the path of morning
To fields where they can play without a quarrel:
A country I'd forgotten, but remember,
And welcome with a cry.

O cool glad pasture; living tree, tall corn,
Great cliff, or languid sloping sand, cold sea,
Waves; rivers curving: you, eternal flowers,
Give me content, while I can think of you:
Give me your living breath!
Back to your rampart, Death.

HAROLD MONRO
'Living', *The Earth for Sale*, 1928

THE happiest part of a man's life is what he
passes lying awake in bed in the morning.

SAMUEL JOHNSON
in Boswell's *Life*, 1791

DAWN CHORUS

THIS morning, lying couched amid the grass
In the deep, deep dingle south of Llangwyth's Pass,
  While it was yet neither quite bright nor dark,
I heard a new and wonderful High Mass.
  The Chief Priest was the nightingale: the lark
And thrush assisted him: and some small bird
  (I do not weet his name) acted as Clerk.
My spirit was lapped in ecstasy: each word,
Word after word, thrilled through me like the deep
Rich music of a dream: not wholly asleep
Nor all awake was I, but, as it were,
  Tranced somewhere between one state and the other.
  All heavy thoughts that through the long day smother
Man's heart and soul with weariness and care
  Were gone, and in their place reigned pure delight.
  The nightingale, sent from a far and bright
Land by my golden sister, prophesied
  Of blessëd days to come, in a sweet voice:
  And the small bird, responding, sang 'Rejoice, rejoice!'
I heard his little bill tinkle and jingle
With a clear silver sound that filled the dingle.
Heaven is a state wherein bliss and devotion mingle,
  And such was mine this morn: I could have died
Of rapture.

DAVID AP GWYLYM (fourteenth century) rendered
by JAMES CLARENCE MANGAN, *Poems*, 1903

APRIL RISE

If ever I saw blessing in the air
  I see it now in this still early day
Where lemon-green the vaporous morning drips
  Wet sunlight on the powder of my eye.

Blown bubble-film of blue, the sky wraps round
  Weeds of warm light whose every root and rod
Splutters with soapy green, and all the world
  Sweats with the bead of summer in its bud.

If ever I heard blessing it is there
  Where birds in trees that shoals and shadows are
Splash with their hidden wings and drops of sound
  Break on my ears their crests of throbbing air.

Pure in the haze the emerald sun dilates,
  The lips of sparrows milk the mossy stones,
While white as water by the lake a girl
  Swims her green hand among the gathered swans.

Now, as the almond burns its smoking wick,
  Dropping small flames to light the candled grass;
Now, as my low blood scales its second chance,
  If ever world were blessed, now it is.

LAURIE LEE, The Bloom of Candles, 1947

RISE AND SHINE

Mr. Salteena awoke next morning in his small but pleasant room. It was done in green and white with Monagrams on the toilit set. He had a tiny white bed with a green quilt and a picture of the Nativity and one of Windsor Castle on the walls. The sun was shining over all these things as Mr. Salteena opened his sleepy eyes. Just then there was a rat tat on the door. Come in called Mr. Salteena and in came Edward Procurio ballancing a tray very cleverly. He looked most elegant with his shiny black hair and pale yellow face and half shut eyes. He smiled in a very mystearious and superior way as he placed the tray on Mr. Salteenas pointed knees.

Your early beverage he announced and began to pull up the blinds still smiling to himself.

O thank you cried Mr. Salteena feeling very towzld compared to this grand fellow. Then to his great supprise Procurio began to open the wardrobe and look at Mr. Salteenas suits making italian exclamations under his breath. Mr. Salteena dare not say a word so he swollowed his tea and eat a Marie biscuit hastilly. Presently Procurio advanced to the bed with a bright blue serge suit. Will you wear this today sir he asked quietly.

Oh certainly said Mr Salteena.

And a clean shirt would not come amiss said Procurio what about this pale blue and white stripe.

With pleashure replied Mr Salteena. So Procurio laid them out in neat array also a razer and brush for shaving. Then he opened a door saying This is the bathroom shall I turn on hot or cold.

I don't mind said Mr Salteena feeling very hot and ignorant.

It is best for you to decide sir said Procurio firmly.

Well I will try cold said Mr Salteena feeling it was more manly to say that. Procurio bowed and beat a retreat to the bath room. Then he returned and told Mr. Salteena that when he was washed he would find his breakfast in the sitting room. When Mr Salteena was dressed in his best blue suit and clean shirt he stroled into the sitting room where a gay canary was singing fit to burst in the window and a copple of doves cooing in a whicker cage. A cheery smell greeted him as Procurio glided in with some steaming coffie. Mr. Salteena felt more at home and passed a few remarks about the weather. Procurio smiled and uncovered some lovely kidnys on toast and as he did so bent and whispered in Mr. Salteenas ear you could have come in in your dressing gown.

Mr Salteena gave a start. Oh can I he said ten thousand thanks.

DAISY ASHFORD, *The Young Visiters*, 1919
(written at the age of nine years)

MORNING GLORY

THE water sparkles as I pour,
Each drop a crystal gem,
Each several drop a gleaming world
Lost in the clear containing glass
Or in the basin lying sleek and still.
What richness!—when a man may slake
His sleepy thirst with precious gems,
And among shining planets plunge his hands.

GERALD BULLETT
New Poems, 1949

OMAN WASHING: PASTEL DRAWING BY EDGAR DEGAS, *c.* 1890

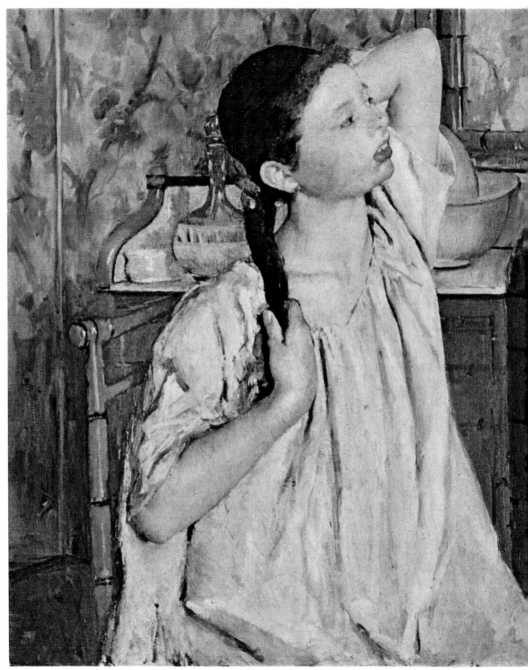

THE MORNING TOILET: PAINTING BY MARY CASSATT, 1886

MORNING

GET up, get up for shame, the blooming morn
Upon her wings presents the god unshorn.
See how Aurora throws her fair
Fresh-quilted colours through the air;
Get up, sweet Slug-a-bed, and see
The dew bespangling herb and tree.
Each flower has wept, and bowed towards the East,
Above an hour since; yet you are not drest,
Nay! not so much as out of bed?
When all the birds have Mattins said,
And sung their thankful hymns: 'tis sin,
Nay, profanation, to keep in,
Whenas a thousand virgins on this day,
Spring, sooner than the lark, to fetch in May.

Rise; and put on your foliage, and be seen
To come forth, like the Spring-time, fresh and green;
And sweet as Flora. Take no care
For jewels for your gown or hair:
Fear not; the leaves will strew
Gems in abundance upon you:
Besides, the childhood of the day has kept,
Against you come, some orient pearls unwept:
Come, and receive them while the light
Hangs on the dew-locks of the night:
And Titan on the Eastern hill
Retires himself, or else stands still
Till you come forth. Wash, dress, be brief in praying:
Few beads are best, when once we go a-Maying.

ROBERT HERRICK, *Hesperides*, 1648

MORNING BATHE: I

... THE rushes blink in quaint surprise,
Wave-startled with a thousand eyes,
And merry blossoms from the grass
Twinkle good morrow as we pass.
Swift down the stream! The silver streak
Curls whispering from the glowing cheek;
O'er curving arm a crystal shower
Crowns the smooth rush of conscious power.
Strong speeds the stroke! Too swift to heed
On wrist and knee the clinging weed;
Through the green tendrils as they part
The deep-seen water-shadows dart;
From willow tree a sapphire gleam
Flames into ruby o'er the stream,
Where Kingfisher, his errand sped,
Leaves murmurs in the lily-bed;
From yew and alder, ripple-clear,
Bright notes break quivering on the ear;
The wren to mock the morning fills
Its sunbeam path with broken trills;
The warbler tosses back one ray
In tumult to the laughing day.
Strong speeds the stroke! In light new born
We leap to catch the kiss of morn;
New hopes salute a summer sky,
New winds of thought shrill gladly by;
Gone is the night and the dusk of showers;
Beauty's awake, and the day is ours!

GEOFFREY WINTHROP YOUNG
Wind and Hill, 1909

MORNING BATHE: II

FROM the geyser ventilators
    Autumn winds are blowing down
On a thousand business women
    Having baths in Camden Town.

Waste pipes chuckle into runnels,
    Steam's escaping here and there,
Morning trains through Camden cutting
    Shake the Crescent and the Square.

Early nip of changeful autumn,
    Dahlias glimpsed through garden doors,
At the back precarious bathrooms
    Jutting out from upper floors.

And behind their frail partitions
    Business women lie and soak,
Seeing through the draughty skylight
    Flying clouds and railway smoke.

Rest you there, poor unbelov'd ones,
    Lap your loneliness in heat.
All too soon the tiny breakfast,
    Trolley-bus and windy street!

JOHN BETJEMAN, 'Business Girls'
A Few Late Chrysanthemums, 1954

AT THE DAWNING OF DAY

THE grey eye of morning was dear to my youth,
  When I sprang like the roe from my bed,
With the glow of the passions, the feelings of truth,
  And the light hand of Time on my head.

For then 'twas my maxim through life to be free,
  And to sport my short moments away;
The cry of the hounds was the music for me,
  My glory—the dawn of the day.

In yellow-leaved autumn the haze of the morn
  Gave promise of rapture to come;
Then melody woke in the sound of the horn,
  As we cheer'd the old fox from his home;

The breeze and the shout met the sun's early beam,
  With the village response in full play;
All vigour, my steed leap'd the fence or the stream,
  And was foremost at dawn of the day.

The well-tuned view-halloo that shook the green wood,
  And arrested the ploughman's gay song,
Gave nerve to the hunters, and fire to the blood
  Of the hounds, as they bounded along.

And shall I relinquish this joy of my heart
  While years with my strength roll away?
Hark! the horn—bring my horse—see, they're ready to start!
  Tally-o! at the dawning of day.

ROBERT BLOOMFIELD, *Remains*, 1824

IVERPOOL PORCELAIN JUG, _c._ 1760

II: GROWING UP

How like an angel came I down!
    How bright are all things here!
When first among his works I did appear
    Oh, how their glory did me crown!
The world resembled his eternity,
    In which my soul did walk;
And everything that I did see
    Did with me talk . . .

A native health and innocence
    Within my bones did grow,
And while my God did all his glories show,
    I felt a vigour in my sense
That was all spirit: I within did flow
    With seas of life like wine;
I nothing in the world did know.
    But 'twas divine . . .

THOMAS TRAHERNE
Poems of Felicity, 1903 (written *c.* 1670)

27

A BOY:
PAINTING BY
CORNELIS DE VOS
(SEVENTEENTH CENTURY)

BLOOM OF YOUTH

FRESH air and liberty are all that is necessary to the happiness of children. In that blissful age 'when nature's self is new,' the bloom of interest and beauty is found alike in every object of perception—in the grass of the meadow, the moss on the rock, and seaweed on the sand. They find gems and treasures in shells and pebbles; and the gardens of fairyland in the simplest flowers. They have no melancholy associations with autumn or with evening. The falling leaves are their playthings; and the setting sun only tells them that they must go to rest as he does, and that he will light them to their sports in the morning. It is this bloom of novelty, and the pure, unclouded, unvitiated feelings with which it is contemplated, that throw such an unearthly radiance on the scenes of our infancy, however humble in themselves, and give a charm to their recollections which not even Tempe can compensate. It is the force of first impressions. The first meadow in which we gather cowslips, the first stream on which we sail, the first home in which we awake to the sense of human sympathy, have all a peculiar and exclusive charm, which we shall never find again in richer meadows, mightier rivers, and more magnificent dwellings; nor even in themselves, when we revisit them after the lapse of years, and the sad realities of noon have dissipated the illusions of sunrise.

THOMAS LOVE PEACOCK, *Melincourt*, 1817

ENRAPTURED EYES

OFT will he witness, with admiring eyes,
The brook's sweet dimples o'er the pebbles rise;
And often, bent as o'er some magic spell,
He'll pause, and pick his shapëd stone and shell:
Raptures the while his inward powers inflame,
And joys delight him which he cannot name.
Ideas picture pleasing views to mind,
For which his language can no utterance find;
Increasing beauties, freshening on his sight,
Unfold new charms, and witness more delight . . .
Thus pausing wild on all he saunters by,
He feels enraptured, though he knows not why;
And hums and mutters o'er his joys in vain,
And dwells on something which he can't explain.
The bursts of thought with which his soul's perplexed
Are bred one moment, and are gone the next;
Yet still the heart will kindling sparks retain,
And thoughts will rise, and Fancy strive again.

JOHN CLARE
from 'Dawnings of Genius'
*Poems Descriptive of Rural Life
and Scenery*, 1820

UNDER THE APPLE BOUGHS

Now as I was young and easy under the apple boughs
About the lilting house and happy as the grass was green,
    The night above the dingle starry,
      Time let me hail and climb
    Golden in the heydays of his eyes,
And honoured among wagons I was prince of the apple towns
And once below a time I lordly had the trees and leaves
      Trail with daisies and barley
    Down the rivers of the windfall light.

And as I was green and carefree, famous among the barns
About the happy yard and singing as the farm was home.
    In the sun that is young once only,
      Time let me play and be
    Golden in the mercy of his means.
And green and golden I was huntsman and herdsman, the calves
Sang to my horn, the foxes on the hills barked clear and cold,
      And the sabbath rang slowly
    In the pebbles of the holy streams.

All the sun long it was running, it was lovely, the hay
Fields high as the house, the tunes from the chimneys, it was air
    And playing, lovely and watery
      And fire green as grass.
    And nightly under the simple stars
As I rode to sleep the owls were bearing the farm away,
All the moon long I heard, blessed among stables, the nightjars
      Flying with the ricks, and the horses
        Flashing into the dark.

And then to awake, and the farm, like a wanderer white
With the dew, come back, the cock on his shoulder: it was all
    Shining, it was Adam and maiden,
        The sky gathered again
    And the sun grew round that very day.
So it must have been after the birth of the simple light
In the first, spinning place, the spellbound horses walking warm
    Out of the whinnying green stable
        On to the fields of praise.

And honoured among foxes and pheasants by the gay house
Under the new made clouds and happy as the heart was long,
    In the sun born over and over,
        I ran my heedless ways,
    My wishes raced through the house high hay
And nothing I cared, at my sky blue trades, that time allows
In all his tuneful turning so few and such morning songs
    Before the children green and golden
        Follow him out of grace.

Nothing I cared, in the lamb white days, that time would take me
Up to the swallow thronged loft by the shadow of my hand,
    In the moon that is always rising,
        Nor that riding to sleep
    I should hear him fly with the high fields
And wake to the farm forever fled from the childless land.
Oh as I was young and easy in the mercy of his means,
        Time held me green and dying
    Though I sang in my chains like the sea.

DYLAN THOMAS, 'Fern Hill'
Deaths and Entrances, 1946

CHILDHOOD ECHOES

                              . . . Many a time,
At evening, when the earliest stars began
To move along the edges of the hills,
Rising or setting, would he stand alone,
Beneath the trees, or by the glimmering lake;
And there, with fingers interwoven, both hands
Pressed closely palm to palm and to his mouth
Uplifted, he, as through an instrument,
Blew mimic hootings to the silent owls,
That they might answer him. And they would shout
Across the water vale, and shout again,
Responsive to his call, with quivering peals,
And long halloos, and screams, and echoes loud
Redoubled and redoubled; concourse wild
Of jocund din! And when a lengthened pause
Of silence came and baffled his best skill,
Then, sometimes, in that silence, while he hung
Listening, a gentle shock of mild surprise
Has carried far into his heart the voice
Of mountain torrents; or the visible scene
Would enter unawares into his mind
With all its solemn imagery, its rocks,
Its woods, and that uncertain heaven, received
Into the bosom of the steady lake.

WILLIAM WORDSWORTH, *The Prelude*, 1850
(written 1799–1805)

WHILOM IN YOUTH . . .

WHILOM in youth, when flowered my joyful spring,
    Like swallow swift I wandered here and there;
For heat of heedless lust me so did sting
    That I of doubted danger had no fear.
        I went the wasteful woods and forests wide
        Withouten dread of wolves to been espied.

I wont to range amid the mazy thicket,
    And gather nuts to make me Christmas game,
And joyëd oft to chase the trembling pricket,
    Or hunt the hartless hare till she were tame.
        What wreakëd I of wintry age's waste?
        Though deemëd I my spring would ever last.

How often have I scaled the craggy oak,
    All to dislodge the raven of her nest;
How have I weariëd with many a stroke
    The stately walnut tree, the while the rest
        Under the tree fell all for nuts at strife?
        For like to me was liberty and life . . .

EDMUND SPENSER
The Shepheardes' Calender, 1579

33

A MERRY COUNTRY LAD

WHO can live in heart so glad
As the merry country lad?
Who upon a fair green balk
May at pleasure sit and walk.
And amid the azure skies
See the morning sun arise;
While he hears in every spring
How the birds do chirp and sing;
Or before the hounds in cry
See the hare go stealing by;
Or along the shallow brook
Angling with a baited hook,
See the fishes leap and play
In a blessed sunny day;
Or to hear the partridge call
Till she have her covey all . . .
Then the bee to gather honey,
And the little black-haired coney
On a bank for sunny place
With her forefeet wash her face:
Are not these, with thousands mo
Than the courts of kings do know,
The true pleasing spirit's sights
That may breed true love's delights?

NICHOLAS BRETON
The Passionate Shepherd, 1604

34

JAMES SAYER FISHING:
PAINTING BY JOHN ZOFFANY, R.A.

LES PEUPLIERS: PAINTING BY CLAUDE MONET, 1890

III : LOOKING

... Look overhead
How air is azurëd;
O how! nay do but stand
Where you can lift your hand
Skywards: rich, rich it laps
Round the four fingergaps ...
Yet such a sapphire-shot,
Charged, steepëd sky will not
Stain light. Yea, mark you this:
It does no prejudice.
The glass-blue days are those
When every colour glows,
Each shape and shadow shows.
Blue be it: this blue heaven
The seven or seven times seven
Hued sunbeam will transmit
Perfect, not alter it.
Or if there does some soft,
On things aloof, aloft,
Bloom breathe, that one breath more
Earth is the fairer for ...

GERARD MANLEY HOPKINS
Poems, 1930 (written 1883)

STARS

IF the stars should appear one night in a thousand years, how would men believe and adore; and preserve for many generations the remembrance of the city of God which had been shown! But every night come out these envoys of beauty, and light the universe with their admonishing smile.

RALPH WALDO EMERSON, *Nature*, 1836

. . . LOOK how the floor of heaven
Is thick inlaid with patines of bright gold!
There's not the smallest orb which thou behold'st
But in his motion like an angel sings
Still quiring to the young-eyed cherubins.

WILLIAM SHAKESPEARE
The Merchant of Venice, 1595

WHEN I survey the bright
   Celestial sphere,
So rich with jewels hung, that night
   Doth like an Ethiop bride appear,
My soul her wings doth spread
   And heavenward flies,
Th' Almighty's mysteries to read
   In the large volumes of the skies . . .

WILLIAM HABINGTON, *Castara*, 1640

MOON

THE light and heat of the sun, like air and water, is a human necessity. The moon is in the nature of a luxury. She is sweetheart rather than wife. She is our night-light. The sun excites, challenges, daunts, dazzles, dazes, may even all but stun the mind with radiance. It sucks self outwards; its heat resembles a fourth skin. In its vast shimmering mantle of gold, it pours life into us.

> With open mouth he drank the sun
> As though it had been wine!

'Doth not the glory of the Sun pay tribute to your sight? Is not the vision of the World an amiable thing?' Not so the moon. Like a spy with a bull's-eye, she silently discloses what she shines upon. She pacifies, invites *us* in. Her light gnaws away shadow; and glides, smooth and softly as a serpent, from stone on to stone. Caught, yet unaware of being so, our instincts and our sentiments are instantly affected by her presence. 'The Sea! the Sea!' we may shout at sight of an ocean basking in splendour beneath the sun; but what barbarian would go bawling into the night to welcome the moon? We tread softly; look and think with caution; as if to be in keeping with this stealthy and motionless lustre. The preternatural is lurking near, is skulking abroad. And a beauty, or bearing, or character in things, indetectable in daylight, now lies in wait for us. Not only is every flower alone in moonlight, and many refuse to bloom until her hour draws near, not only is the air sweet and heavy with smells and odours, and every rose chilled with dew resembles a rose dreaming of itself; but even so gross and coarse a plant as the vegetable marrow, when its great thorny leaves are dusked over with the moon's silver, becomes not only singularly beautiful, but as individual an organism as a basking alligator.

WALTER DE LA MARE, *Behold, this Dreamer!* 1939

THE NARROW PERSPECTIVE

GOD is glorified in the sun and moon, in the rare fabric of the honeycombs, in the discipline of bees, in the economy of pismires, in the little houses of birds, in the curiosity of an eye, God being pleased to delight in those little images and reflexes of himself from those pretty mirrors, which like a crevice in a wall through a narrow perspective transmit the species of a vast excellency . . .

JEREMY TAYLOR, *Twenty-eight Sermons*, 1651

PLEASURES lie thickest where no pleasures seem;
There's not a leaf that falls upon the ground
But holds some joy, of silence or of sound,
Some sprite begotten of a summer dream.
The very meanest things are made supreme
With innate ecstasy. No grain of sand
But moves a bright and million-peopled land,
And hath its Edens and its Eves, I deem.

SAMUEL LAMAN BLANCHARD, *Lyric Offerings*, 1828

THERE is not so poor a creature, but may be thy glass to see God in. The greatest flat glass that can be made cannot represent anything greater than it is. If every gnat that flies were an Archangel, all that could but tell me that there is a God; and the poorest worm that creeps tells me that.

JOHN DONNE, *Eighty Sermons*, 1640

THE sweetest essences are always confined in the smallest glasses.

JOHN DRYDEN, Dedication of the *Aeneis*, 1697

FLOWERS AND INSECTS: PAINTING BY ROELANDT SAVERY, 1611

THE MO...
PAINTIN...
JOHN NA...
c. 1922

LANDSCAPE

I WALK of grey noons by the old canal
  Where rain-drops patter on the autumn leaves
Now watching from some ivied orchard wall
  In slopes of stubble figures pile the sheaves;
Or under banks in shadow of their grass,
Blue water-flies by starts jettingly pass
'Mid large leaves level on the glassy cool;
  Or noiseless dizzy midges winking round
The yellow sallows of the meadow pool;
  While into cloudy silence ebbs each sound,
And sifts the moulting sunlight warm and mellow
  O'er sandy beach remote, or slumberous flood,
  Or rooky, red brick mansion by the wood,
Mossed gate, or farmyard hay-stacks tanned and yellow.

THOMAS CAULFIELD IRWIN
Sonnets on the Poetry and Problems of Life, 1881

POINTS OF VIEW

BY the very right of your senses you enjoy the world. Is not the beauty of the Hemisphere present to your eye? Doth not the glory of the sun pay tribute to your sight? Is not the vision of the world an amiable thing? Do not the stars shed influences to perfect the air?

THOMAS TRAHERNE
Centuries of Meditations, 1908 (written *c.* 1670)

THE tree which moves some to tears of joy is in the eyes of others only a green thing which stands in the way . . . As a man is, so he sees.

WILLIAM BLAKE
in a letter to the Rev. Dr. Trusler, 1799

To a lady who, looking at an engraving of a house, called it an ugly thing, he said, 'No, madam, there is nothing ugly; I never saw an ugly thing in my life: for let the form of an object be what it may—light, shade, and perspective will always make it beautiful.'

JOHN CONSTABLE
quoted in C. R. LESLIE's *Life*, 1843

WHEN the act of reflection takes place in the mind, when we look at ourselves in the light of thought, we discover that our life is embosomed in beauty. Behind us, as we go, all things assume pleasing forms, as clouds do far off. Not only things familiar and stale, but even the tragic and terrible, are comely, as they take their place in the pictures of memory. The river-bank, the weed at the water-side, the old house, the foolish person—however neglected in the passing—have a grace in the past.

RALPH WALDO EMERSON, 'Spiritual Laws,' *Essays*, 1847

A DISCOVERER

To be with Lawrence was a kind of adventure, a voyage of discovery into newness and otherness. For, being himself of a different order, he inhabited a different universe from that of common men—a brighter and intenser world, of which, while he spoke, he would make you free. He looked at things with the eyes, so it seemed, of a man who had been at the brink of death and to whom, as he emerges from the darkness, the world reveals itself as unfathomably beautiful and mysterious. For Lawrence, existence was one continuous convalescence; it was as though he were newly re-born from a mortal illness every day of his life. What these convalescent eyes saw his most casual speech would reveal. A walk with him in the country was a walk through that marvellously rich and significant landscape which is at once the background and the principal personage of all his novels. He seemed to know, by personal experience, what it was like to be a tree or a daisy or a breaking wave or even the mysterious moon itself. He could get inside the skin of an animal and tell you in the most convincing detail how it felt and how, dimly, inhumanly, it thought. Of Black-Eyed Susan, for example, the cow at his New Mexican ranch, he was never tired of speaking, nor was I ever tired of listening to his account of her character and her bovine philosophy.

'He sees', Vernon Lee once said to me, 'more than a human being ought to see. Perhaps,' she added, 'that's why he hates humanity so much.' Why also he loved it so much. And not only humanity: nature too, and even the supernatural. For wherever he looked, he saw more than a human being ought to see; saw more and therefore loved and hated more. To be with him was to find oneself transported to one of the frontiers of human consciousness.

ALDOUS HUXLEY
The Letters of D. H. Lawrence, 1932

45

EARTH'S EMBROIDERY

For if delight may provoke men's labour, what greater delight is there than to behold the earth apparalled with plants, as with a robe of embroidered work, set with Orient pearls and garnished with great diversity of rare and costly jewels? If this variety and perfection of colours may affect the eye, it is such in herbs and flowers that no Apelles, no Zeuxis, ever could by any art express the like: if odours or if taste may work satisfaction they are both so sovereign in plants and so comfortable that no confection of the apothecaries can equal their excellent virtue. But these delights are in the outward senses; the principal delight is in the mind, singularly enriched with the knowledge of these visible things, setting forth to us the invisible wisdom and admirable workmanship of Almighty God.

JOHN GERARD, from the
Dedication of his *Herbal*, 1597

GEMS AND JEWELS

THIS evening my wife did with great pleasure shew me her stock of jewels, increased by the ring she hath made lately as my Valentine's gift this year, a Turkey stone set with diamonds; and, with this and what she had, she reckons that she hath above £150 worth of jewels, of one kind or other; and I am glad of it, for it is fit the wretch should have something to content herself with.

SAMUEL PEPYS, *Diary*
February 23, 1668

THE lining of my waistcoat pockets is always getting tattered, like my soul, by little ornaments, little idols, and by beautiful fragments of all sorts: A Greek intaglio ring with the figure of Mercury—bought for forty silver shekels—rubs up against an old wedding-ring with the piquant old English motto 'My hart and I untill I dy'; a tiny scrap of black opal—my lucky month's stone; a little lost pearl which had been picked up under the counter; a Renaissance ring, showing Cupid lying bound in chains, in a crystal cage; a Roman ring depicting a Roman soldier treading on a Jewish captive; a little bit of engraved glass, showing a black slave on his knees, pleading: 'Am I, then, not a man and a brother?' along with a little lost key, and a poor, perspiring bit of lead-pencil. And under the fluff and ragged ends of the lining an emerald is always playing at blind-man's buff with a little moonstone.

MOYSHEH OYVED, *Visions and Jewels*, 1925

KISSING your hand may make you feel very very good but a diamond and safire bracelet lasts forever.

ANITA LOOS, *Gentlemen Prefer Blondes*, 1925

47

DEW

SEE how the Orient dew,
Shed from the bosom of the morn
   Into the blowing roses,
Yet careless of its mansion new—
For the clear region where t'was born
   Round in itself encloses
And, in its little globe's extent,
Frames as it can its native element—
     How it the purple flower does slight,
       Scarce touching where it lies,
     But, gazing back upon the skies,
       Shines with a mournful light,
Like its own tear,
Because so long divided from the Sphere.

Restless it rolls, and unsecure,
Trembling lest it grow impure,
Till the warm sun pity its pain,
And to the skies exhale it back again.
So the soul, that drop, that ray
Of the clear fountain of eternal day,
     Could it within the human flower be seen,
       Remembering still its former height,
     Shuns the sweet leaves and blossoms green,
       And, recollecting its own light,
Does, in its pure and circling thoughts, express
The greater heaven in a heaven less.

ANDREW MARVELL
Miscellaneous Poems, 1681

AN ENCHANTED GARDEN

I SHALL never forget my surprise and delight on first beholding the bottom of the sea . . . The water within the reef was as calm as a pond; and, as there was no wind, it was quite clear, from the surface to the bottom, so that we could see down easily even at a depth of twenty or thirty yards. When Jack and I dived into shallower water, we expected to have found sand and stones, instead of which we found ourselves in what appeared really to be an enchanted garden. The whole of the bottom of the lagoon, as we called the calm water within the reef, was covered with coral of every shape, size and hue. Some portions were formed like large mushrooms; others appeared like the brain of a man, having stalks or necks attached to them; but the most common kind was a species of branching coral, and some portions were of a lovely pale pink colour, others were pure white. Among this there grew large quantities of sea-weed of the richest hues imaginable, and of the most graceful forms; while innumerable fishes—blue, red, yellow, green and striped—sported in and out among the flower-beds of this submarine garden.

R. M. BALLANTYNE, *The Coral Island*, 1860

ANOTHER ENCHANTED GARDEN

I LOVE a still conservatory
    That's full of giant, breathless palms,
Azaleas, clematis and vines,
    Whose quietness great Trees becalms
Filling the air with foliage,
    A curved and dreamy statuary.

I love to hear a cold, pure rill
    Of water trickling low, afar
With sudden little jerks and purls
    Into a tank or stoneware jar,
The song of a tiny sleeping bird
    Held like a shadow in its trill.

I love the mossy quietness
    That grows upon the great stone flags,
The dark tree-ferns, the staghorn ferns,
    The prehistoric, antlered stags
That carven stand and stare among
    The silent, ferny wilderness.

And are they birds or souls that flit
    Among the trees so silently?
And are they fish or ghosts that haunt
    The still pools of the rockery?
For I am but a sculptured rock
    As in that magic place I sit . . .

I watch a white Nyanza float
    Upon a green, untroubled pool,
A fairyland Ophelia, she
    Has cast herself in water cool,
And lies while fairy cymbals ring
    Drowned in her fairy castle moat.

The goldfish sing a winding song
    Below her pale and waxen face,
The water-nymph is dancing by
    Lifting smooth arms with mournful grace,
A stainless white dream she floats on
    While fairies beat a fairy gong.

Silent the Cattleyas blaze
    And thin red orchid shapes of Death
Peer savagely with twisted lips
    Sucking an eerie, phantom breath
With that bright, spotted, fever'd lust
    That watches lonely travellers craze.

Gigantic, mauve and hairy leaves
    Hang like obliterated faces
Full of dim unattained expression
    Such as haunts virgin forest places
When Silence leaps among the trees
    And the echoing heart deceives.

W. J. TURNER
'Magic', *The Hunter*, 1916

ALONE IN A WOOD

IT was still almost summer in the heart of the wood; and as soon as I had scrambled through the hedge, I found myself in a dim green forest atmosphere under eaves of virgin foliage. In places where the wood had itself for a background and the trees were massed together thickly, the colour became intensified and almost gem-like: a perfect fire of green, that seemed none the less green for a few specks of autumn gold. None of the trees were of any considerable age or stature; but they grew well together, I have said; and as the road turned and wound among them, they fell into pleasant groupings and broke the light up pleasantly. Sometimes there would be a colonnade of slim, straight tree-stems with the light running down them as down the shafts of pillars, that looked as if it ought to lead to something, and led only to a corner of sombre and intricate jungle. Sometimes a spray of delicate foliage would be thrown out flat, the light lying flatly along the top of it, so that against a dark background it seemed almost luminous. There was a great hush over the thicket (for indeed, it was more of a thicket than a wood); and the vague rumours that went among the tree-tops, and the occasional rustling of big birds or hares among the under-growth, had in them a note of almost treacherous stealthiness, that put the imagination on its guard and made me walk warily on the russet carpet of last year's leaves. The spirit of the place seemed to be all attention; the wood listened as I went, and held its breath to number my footfalls.

ROBERT LOUIS STEVENSON, from 'An Autumn Effect'
Essays of Travel, 1905 (written 1875)

EYES OF THE EARTH

PASSIVE I lie, looking up through leaves,
An eye only, one of the eyes of earth
That open at a myriad points at the living surface.
Eyes that earth opens see and delight
Because of the leaves, because of the unfolding of the leaves.
The folding, veining, imbrication, fluttering, resting,
The green and deepening manifold of the leaves.

Eyes of the earth know only delight
Untroubled by anything that I am, and I am nothing:
All that nature is, receive and recognize,
Pleased with the sky, the falling water and the flowers,
With bird and fish and the striations of stone.
Every natural form, living and moving
Delights these eyes that are no longer mine
That open upon earth and sky pure vision.
Nature sees, sees itself, is both seer and seen.

This is the divine repose, that watches
The ever-changing light and shadow, rock and sky and ocean.

KATHLEEN RAINE
'Seventh Day', *The Year One*, 1952

IN THE DEPTHS

THE cavern shrank again, the walls almost touched, and the ceiling seemed to join the floor. The remaining passage was a regular cat-hole, and we had to wriggle in in true cat fashion. We bowed one another in as if in a drawing-room; M. Catala was the first to go through, flat on his stomach. He crawled laboriously, while the rest of us waited anxiously with our heads together and our lamps on the ground. His feet disappeared; we heard the rubbing of cloth, the grating of hobnails on the stone, a stifled groan. Finally there was a moment's silence while he stood up and pointed his light ahead. The next sign of life was a roar of astonished triumph; finally we heard him shout through the tunnel: 'The white sea!'

His words recalled one of the most extraordinary scenes in my old favourite, Verne's *Journey to the Centre of the Earth*. I flung myself into the tunnel, and scrambled out at the other end, followed by the rest of the party.

A white, brilliant, coagulated surface spread out under our feet; it was terminated by high cliffs, also white. Nowhere but under-ground could we have seen such a spectacle. This smooth, unbroken expanse was neither water nor ice; it was a floor of moist, shiny stalagmite. The walls were covered with a dull, granular deposit, deceptively like the sides of an ice-floe.

The frozen sea rang under our feet as we walked. The whole thing was so like a polar scene that we thought we felt a chill breeze. So we did, in fact; it was not an illusion. The resemblance was unimaginably perfect. We walked Indian file through an arctic wilderness, and the unreal, diffuse light of our lamps must have been like that of the midnight sun. To cap it all, the stalagmite cracked and gave under my weight, and my leg sank in as I jumped away. I returned cautiously to the gaping hole; it was full of clear water, of the turquoise cast peculiar to glaciers.

If I had been alone when I saw these marvels, I would hardly dare describe them now for fear of sceptical smiles. But the absolute stupefaction of my companions is a sign that I am not exaggerating. And there were yet more astonishing things to come.

The white sea narrowed to a winding fjord between beetling cliffs; then the surface rose to the foot of a petrified waterfall. Beyond, the gallery continued narrow; its walls were covered with a spiny deposit which hooked and scratched the would-be passer-by. We scrambled up an abrupt rise out of the corridor into a spacious chamber.

Here we stood speechless. Just when we thought we had exhausted our powers of admiration, we stepped into a fairy palace. Hundreds of caverns and countless strange stories and pictures had not prepared me for marvels like these.

Stalactites and crystals sparkled everywhere; their profusion, their whiteness, their shapes were fantastic beyond belief. We were inside a precious stone; it was a palace of crystal. But that is a mere cliché for what we saw. I will not pile up superlatives by attempting a general description. Even in colouring and delicacy the formations surpassed the most gorgeous flowers of nature.

There were microscopic stalactites and flawlessly transparent giant crystals. There were shiny formations, dull formations, smooth formations, spiny formations, milky, red, black, crude green formations. The colours came from mineral infiltrations, of which the mountain has a rich and varied store. Finally, there were two entirely new phenomena, still unexplained: huge needles as fine as cobwebs, which trembled and broke at a breath, and silver strings with the brilliance of silk yarn, which dangled from roof and walls.

NORBERT CASTERET, *Ten Years Under the Earth*, translated by Barrows Mussey, 1939

VENETIAN VIEWS

                   . . . THE hoar
And aery Alps towards the North appeared
Through mist, an heaven-sustaining bulwark reared
Between the East and West; and half the sky
Was roofed with clouds of rich emblazonry
Dark purple at the zenith, which still grew
Down the steep West into a wondrous hue
Brighter than burning gold, even to the rent
Where the swift sun yet paused in his descent
Among the many-folded hills: they were
Those famous Euganean hills, which bear,
As seen from Lido thro' the harbour piles,
The likeness of a clump of peakëd isles—
And then—as if the Earth and Sea had been
Dissolved into one lake of fire, were seen
Those mountains towering as from waves of flame
Around the vaporous sun, from which there came
The inmost purple spirit of light, and made
Their very peaks transparent. 'Ere it fade,'
Said my companion, 'I will show you soon
A better station'—so, o'er the lagune
We glided; and from that funereal bark
I leaned, and saw the city, and could mark
How from their many isles, in evening's gleam,
Its temples and its palaces did seem
Like fabrics of enchantment piled to Heaven.

PERCY BYSSHE SHELLEY
from 'Julian and Maddalo'
Posthumous Poems, 1824 (written in 1818)

FAIR, FANTASTIC PARIS

So, I mused
Up and down, up and down, the terraced streets,
The glittering boulevards, the white colonnades
Of fair fantastic Paris who wears boughs
Like plumes, as if man made them, spire and tower
As if they had grown by nature, tossing up
Her fountains in the sunshine of the squares,
As if in beauty's game she tossed the dice,
Or blew the silver down-balls of her dreams,
To sow futurity with seeds of thought
And count the passage of her festive hours.

The city swims in verdure, beautiful
As Venice on the waters, the sea-swan.
What bosky gardens, dropped in close-walled courts,
Like plums in ladies' laps, who start and laugh;
What miles of streets that run on after trees,
Still carrying all the necessary shops,
Those open caskets, with the jewels seen!
And trade is art, and art's philosophy,
In Paris.

ELIZABETH BARRETT BROWNING
Aurora Leigh, 1857

NAVAL VIEWS

IN going across the harbour we passed close under the stern of the old *Royal George*. It was the first time I ever floated on salt water; the first hundred-gun ship I ever saw. Ye gods! what a sight—what a sensation! ... It is impossible to forget the breathless astonishment and delight with which my eyes were fixed upon this ship. Nothing so exquisitely touching has ever occurred to me since to produce the same frantic joy. After the first exclamation of ecstasy I for a time spoke not a word; overwhelmed by a thousand feelings, and almost motionless, until presently, as we approached nearer to the *Royal George*, and went closely under her richly carved stern, I broke into a rapid succession of questions, and almost springing out of the hands of the strokesman of the boat, who held me as I stood upon the seat, I was told I should tumble into the sea if I was not quiet....

ADMIRAL SIR THOMAS BYAM MARTIN, *Journal*, 1781

Is she not beautiful? reposing there
  On her own shadow, with her white wings furled;
Moveless, as in the sleepy sunny air,
  Rests the meek swan in her own quiet world.

Is she not beautiful? her graceful bow
  Triumphant rising o'er th' enamour'd tides
That, glittering in the noon-day sunbeam, now
  Just leap and die along her polished sides ...

NOEL THOMAS CARRINGTON
My Native Village and Other Poems, 1830

ELSON'S FLAGSHIPS (DETAIL): PAINTING BY NICHOLAS POCOCK, 1807

LE CONCERT: SEVENTEENTH-CENTURY FRENCH TAPESTRY

IV : LISTENING

MUSIC is a roaring-meg against melancholy, to rear and revive the languishing soul; affecting not only the ears, but the very arteries, the vital and animal spirits, it erects the mind and makes it nimble. This it will effect in the most dull, severe, and sorrowful souls, expel grief with mirth; and, if there be any clouds, dust, or dregs of cares yet lurking in our thoughts, most powerfully it wipes them all away, and that which is more, it will perform all this in an instant—cheer up the countenance, expel austerity, bring in hilarity, inform our manners, mitigate anger . . . Many other properties Cassiodorus reckons up of this our divine music, not only to expel the greatest griefs, but it doth extenuate fears and furies, appeaseth cruelty, abateth heaviness; and to such as are watchful, it causeth quiet rest; it takes away spleen and hatred, be it instrumental, vocal, with strings, wind . . . it cures all irksomeness and heaviness of the soul. Labouring men that sing to their work can tell as much; and so can soldiers when they go to fight, whom terror of death cannot so much affright, as the sound of trumpet, drum, fife, and such like music, animates . . . It makes a child quiet, the nurse's song; and many times the sound of a trumpet on a sudden, bells ringing, a carman's whistle, a boy singing some ballad tune early in the street, alters, revives, recreates a restless patient that cannot sleep in the night, etc. In a word, it is so powerful a thing that it ravisheth the soul, *regina sensuum*, the queen of the senses, by sweet pleasure (which is an happy cure); and corporal tunes pacify our incorporeal soul: *sine ore loquens, dominatum in animam exercet*, and carries it beyond itself, helps, elevates, extends it.

ROBERT BURTON, *The Anatomy of Melancholy*, 1621

WHEN MUSIC SOUNDS...

WHEN music sounds, gone is the earth I know,
And all her lovely things even lovelier grow;
Her flowers in vision flame, her forest trees
Lift burdened branches, stilled with ecstasies.

When music sounds, out of the water rise
Naiads whose beauty dims my waking eyes,
Rapt in strange dream burns each enchanted face,
With solemn echoing stirs their dwelling-place.

When music sounds, all that I was I am
Ere to this haunt of brooding dust I came;
And from Time's woods break into distant song
The swift-winged hours, as I hasten along.

WALTER DE LA MARE, *Motley*, 1918

HARMONY

WHEN whispering strains, with creeping wind,
   Distil soft passion through the heart;
And when at every touch we find
   Our pulses beat and bear a part;
      When threads can make
      A heart-string shake,
      Philosophy
      Can not deny
Our souls consist of harmony.

When unto heavenly joys, we feign
   Whate'er the soul affecteth most,
Which only thus we can explain,
   By music of the heavenly host,
      Whose lays, methinks,
      Make stars to shrink,
      Philosophy
      May judge thereby
Our souls consist of harmony.

Oh, lull me, lull me, charming air!
   My senses rock with wonder sweet;
Like snow on wool thy fallings are,
   Soft as a spirit's are thy feet;
      Grief who need fear
      That hath an ear?
      Down let him lie
      And slumbering die,
And change his soul for harmony.

WILLIAM STRODE, in *The Academy of Compliments*, 1650

FUGUE

First you deliver your phrase
  —Nothing propound, that I see,
Fit in itself for much blame or much praise—
  Answered no less, where no answer needs be;
Off start the Two on their ways!

Straight must a Third interpose,
  Volunteer needlessly help—
In strikes a Fourth, a Fifth thrusts in his nose,
  So the cry's open, the kennel's a-yelp.
Argument's hot to the close!

One dissertates, he is candid—
  Two must discept,—has distinguished!
Three helps the couple, if ever yet man did;
  Four protests, Five makes a dart at the thing wished—
Back on One, goes the case bandied!

One says his say with a difference—
  More of expounding, explaining!
All now is wrangle, abuse, and vociferance—
  Now there's a truce, all's subdued, self-restraining
Five, though, stands out all the stiffer hence.

One is incisive, corrosive;
  Two retorts, nettled, curt, crepitant;
Three makes rejoinder, expansive, explosive;
  Four overbears them all, strident and strepitant:
Five . . . O Danaides, O Sieve!

Now, they ply axes and crowbars—
    Now, they prick pins at a tissue
Fine as a skein of the casuist Escobar's
    Worked on the bone of a lie. To what issue?
Where is our gain at the Two-bars?

Est fuga, volvitur rota!
    On we drift. Where looms the dim port?
One, Two, Three, Four, Five, contribute their quota—
    Something is gained, if one caught but the import—
Show it us, Hugues of Saxe-Gotha!

What with affirming, denying,
    Holding, riposting, subjoining,
All's like . . . it's like . . . for an instance I'm trying . . .
    There! See our roof, its gilt moulding and groining
Under those spider-webs lying!

So your fugue broadens and thickens,
    Greatens and deepens and lengthens,
Till one exclaims—'But where's music, the dickens?
    Blot ye the gold, while your spider-web strengthens,
Blacked to the stoutest of tickens?' . . .

ROBERT BROWNING
from 'Master Hugues of Saxe-Gotha'
Dramatic Lyrics, 1842

'AN DIE MUSIK' WORDS BY FRANZ VON SCHOB

Herz   zu war-mer Lieb' ent-zunden,   hast mich in ei—ne
beß'—rer Zeiten mir er-schlossen,   du hol—de Kunst, ich

beß'—re Welt entrückt,   in eine beß'—re Welt entrückt!
danke dir da-für,   du holde Kunst, ich dan—ke dir!

2nd verse

USIC BY FRANZ SCHUBERT

67

A VOICE

YOUR voice, that's ravishing, so rare,
It moves the Cerean panting air,
And makes the woods to walk;
Hard-hearted rocks are moved to tears,
And earth doth stretch her porous ears,
Rivers leave murmuring talk.

The sun so ravished in his ear
As will not leave thy hemisphere;
The fixëd stars now move,
And all the planets have no choice
But now are fixëd by thy voice:
Thus all is turned to love.

Hard minerals now liquid flow,
Swelled hills fall into valleys low,
Amazed where you do come;
The wilder beasts tame, void of fears,
And all man's senses turned to ears,
The twatling echo dumb.

WILLIAM CAVENDISH,
DUKE OF NEWCASTLE
The Phanseys, c. 1645

BIRD SONG

O BIRDS, my brothers, sing to me once more
E'er I return again to whence I came,
Give me your joy, your innocence, your lore,
Your air-born, wind-blown ecstasy I claim
Because ye truly are my brothers dear,
Sing to me once again before I go from here. . . .
The joyful song that welcomes in the spring,
The tender mating song so bravely shy,
The song that builds the nest, the merry ring
When the long wait is ended and ye bring
The young birds out and teach them how to fly:
Sing to me of the beechnuts on the ground,
And of the first wild flight at early dawn,
And of the store of berries someone found
And hid away until ye gathered round
And ate them while he shrieked upon the lawn:
Sing of the swinging nest upon the tree,
And of your mates who call and hide away,
And of the sun that shines exceedingly,
And of the leaves that dance, and all the glee
And rapture that begins at break of day . . .

JAMES STEPHENS, from 'A Prelude and a Song',
The Hill of Vision, 1912

THE CHIME OF THE SEA

CONSIDER the sea's listless chime:
   Time's self it is, made audible,
   The murmur of the earth's own shell.
Secret continuance sublime
   Is the sea's end: our sight may pass
   No furlong further. Since time was,
This sound hath told the lapse of time.

No quiet, which is death's,—it hath
   The mournfulness of ancient life,
   Enduring always at dull strife.
As the world's heart of rest and wrath,
   Its painful pulse is in the sands.
   Last utterly, the whole sky stands,
Grey and not known, along its path . . .

Gather a shell from the strown beach
   And listen at its lips: they sigh
   The same desire and mystery,
The echo of the whole sea's speech.
   And all mankind is thus at heart
   Not anything but what thou art:
And Earth, Sea, Man, are all in each.

DANTE GABRIEL ROSSETTI
from 'The Sea's Limits,' *Poems*, 1870

V: EATING AND DRINKING

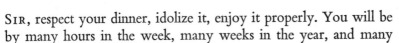

SIR, respect your dinner, idolize it, enjoy it properly. You will be by many hours in the week, many weeks in the year, and many years in your life, the happier if you do.

Don't tell me it is not worthy of a man. All a man's senses are worthy of employment, and should be cultivated as a duty. The senses are the arts. What glorious feasts does Nature prepare for your eye in animal form, in landscape and in painting! Are you to put out your eyes and not see? What royal dishes does her bounty provide for you in the shape of poetry, music, whether windy or wiry, notes of the human voice, or ravishing songs of birds! Are you to stuff your ears with cotton, and vow that the sense of hearing is unmanly? —you obstinate dolt you! No, surely; nor must you be so absurd as to fancy that the art of eating is in any way less worthy than the other two. You like your dinner, man! never be ashamed to say so. If you don't like your victuals, pass on to the next article; but remember that every man who has been worth a fig in this world as poet, painter, or musician, has had a good appetite, and a good taste.

WILLIAM MAKEPEACE THACKERAY
'Memorials of Gormandising'
in *Fraser's Magazine*, June 1841

WINE

WINE by its moisture quencheth my thirst, whether I consider it or no: but to see it flowing from His love who gave it unto man quencheth the thirst even of the Holy Angels. To consider it is to drink it spiritually. To rejoice in its diffusion is to be of a public mind. And to take pleasure in all the benefits it doth to all is Heavenly, for so they do in Heaven.

THOMAS TRAHERNE
Centuries of Meditations, 1908 (written *c.* 1670)

'TIS thou, above nectar, O divinest soul!
(Eternal in thyself) that canst control
That which subverts whole nature, grief and care,
Vexation of the mind and damn'd despair.
'Tis thou alone who by thy mystic fan
Work'st more than wisdom, art or nature can,
To rouse the sacred madness, and awake
The frost-bound blood and spirits . . .

Thou mak'st me airy, active to be borne,
Like Iphyclus, upon the tops of corn.
Thou mak'st me nimble, as the wingèd hours,
To dance and caper on the heads of flowers,
And ride the sunbeams. Can there be a thing
Under the heavenly Isis that can bring
More love unto my life, or can present
My genius with a fuller blandishment?

ROBERT HERRICK, *Hesperides*, 1648

FRUGAL FARE

HE [Mr. Harry Chaplin] placed high among the pleasures of the table, as every true *gourmet* does, victuals of plain perfection. Lady Radnor and he and I were once strolling after lunch on Sunday in her kitchen garden at Cookham, and he observed a fine row of broad beans. 'My Dear,' he said to her, 'those look excellent beans. Do tell your gardener to send some into the house, and let us have beans and bacon for dinner. There's nothing in the world so good.' The gardener was off duty, as it was Sunday afternoon, but she said that if he cared to pick them, and bring them to the house, he should have his dish. So off came his hat, and we filled it with bean pods, and carried it in triumph to the cook, and Mr. Harry said that he would have beans and bacon for dinner, and nothing else whatever; he could not imagine a more delicious dinner. But then the *gourmet* had a word to say to that, for when dinner-time came, he first refused soup, but then discovered that it had a most attractive aroma, and said he would just have 'a spoonful of soup', which meant an ordinary helping for a grown man. Some fish was then placed before him, and he ate his fish in an absent-minded manner, almost mournfully, in fact, for it was salmon, and it reminded him of a heavy fish he had lost on the Brora. Then, so suitably for this hot evening, there was some cold pressed beef (for he remembered how excellent his sister's pressed beef always was) and a mouthful of chicken. Then naturally he must eat the beans and bacon which had been provided specially for him, and so he had two helpings of them, and said he had never tasted such excellent beans, and the bacon was very good too—where did she get it?

E. F. BENSON, *As We Were*, 1930

73

EDWARDIAN BREAKFAST

THE smell of last night's port had given place to the smell of this morning's spirits of wine. Rows of little spirit lamps warmed rows of large silver dishes. On a table to the right between the windows were grouped Hams, Tongues, Galantines, Cold Grouse, ditto Pheasant, ditto Partridge, ditto Ptarmigan. No Edwardian meal was complete without Ptarmigan. Hot or cold. Just Ptarmigan. There would also be a little delicate rectangle of pressed beef from the shop of M. Benoist. On a further table, to the left between the doors, stood fruits of different calibre, and jugs of cold water, and jugs of lemonade. A fourth table contained porridge utensils. A fifth coffee, and pots of Indian and China tea. The latter were differentiated from each other by little ribbons of yellow (indicating China) and of red (indicating, without *arrière pensée*, our Indian Empire). The centre table, which was prepared for twenty-three people, would be bright with Malmaisons and toast-racks. No newspapers were, at that stage, allowed . . .

Edwardian breakfasts were in no sense a hurried proceeding. The porridge was disposed of negligently, people walking about and watching the rain descend upon the Italian garden. Then would come whiting and omelette and devilled kidneys and little fishy messes in shells. And then tongue and ham and a slice of Ptarmigan. And then scones and honey and marmalade. And then a little melon, and a nectarine or two, and just one or two of those delicious raspberries. The men at that stage would drift (I employ the accepted term) to the smoking room. The women would idle in the saloon watching the rain descend upon the Italian garden. It was then 10.30.

SIR HAROLD NICOLSON, *Small Talk*, 1937

LUNCH IN OXBRIDGE

THE lunch on this occasion began with soles, sunk in a deep dish, over which the college cook had spread a counterpane of the whitest cream, save that it was branded here and there with brown spots like the spots on the flanks of a doe. After that came the partridges, but if this suggests a couple of bald, brown birds on a plate you are mistaken. The partridges, many and various, came with all their retinue of sauces and salads, the sharp and the sweet, each in its order; their potatoes, thin as coins but not so hard; their sprouts, foliated as rosebuds but more succulent. And no sooner had the roast and its retinue been done with than the silent serving-man, the Beadle himself perhaps in a milder manifestation, set before us, wreathed in napkins, a confection which rose all sugar from the waves. To call it pudding and so relate it to rice and tapioca would be an insult. Meanwhile the wineglasses had flushed yellow and flushed crimson; had been emptied; had been filled. And thus by degrees was lit, halfway down the spine, which is the seat of the soul, not that hard little electric light which we call brilliance, as it pops in and out upon our lips, but the more profound, subtle and subterranean glow which is the rich yellow flame of rational intercourse. No need to hurry. No need to sparkle. No need to be anybody but oneself. We are all going to heaven and Vandyck is of the company—in other words, how good life seemed, how sweet its rewards, how trivial this grudge or that grievance, how admirable friendship and the society of one's kind, as, lighting a good cigarette, one sunk among the cushions in the window-seat.

VIRGINIA WOOLF, *A Room of One's Own*, 1929

CAROLEAN DINNER

My poor wife rose by five o'clock in the morning, before day, and went to market and bought fowls and many other things for dinner, with which I was highly pleased; and the chine of beef was down also before six o'clock, and my own jack, of which I was doubtful, do carry it very well. Things being put in order, and the cook come, I went to the office, where we sat till noon and then broke up, and I home; whither by and by comes Dr Clerke and his lady, his sister and a she-cousin, and Mr Pierce and his wife; which was all my guests. I had for them, after oysters, at first course a hash of rabbits, a lamb, and a rare chine of beef. Next a great dish of roasted fowl, cost me about 30s., and a tart; then fruit and cheese. My dinner was noble and enough. I had my house mighty clean and neat; my room below with a good fire in it; my dining-room above, and my chamber being made a withdrawing-chamber; and my wife's a good fire also. I find my new table very proper, and will hold nine or ten people well, but eight with great room. After dinner the women to cards in my wife's chamber, and the Dr and Mr Pierce in mine, because the dining-room smokes unless I keep a good charcoal fire, which I was not then provided with. At night to supper, had a good sack posset and cold meat, and sent my guests away about ten o'clock at night, both them and myself highly pleased with our management of this day; and indeed their company was very fine, and Mrs Clerke a very witty, fine lady, though a little conceited and proud. So weary, so to bed. I believe this day's feast will cost me near £5.

SAMUEL PEPYS, *Diary*, 13 January 1663

PEWTER, CHINA AND GLAS
PAINTING BY J. J. TRECK, 16

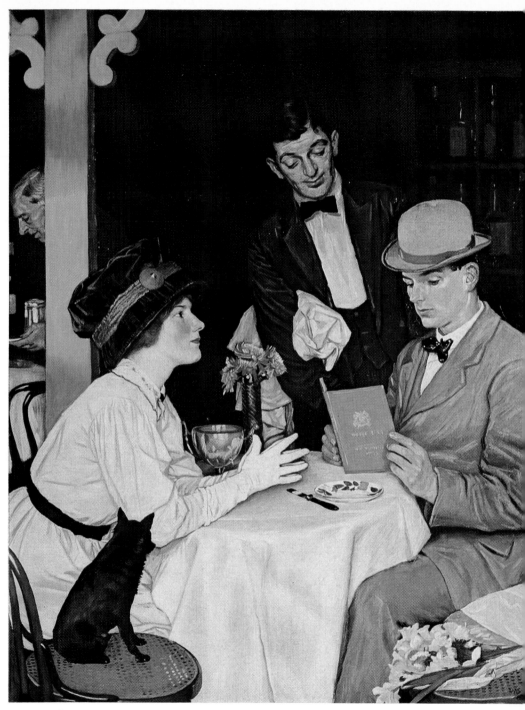

BANK HOLIDAY: PAINTING BY WILLIAM STRANG, R.A., 1912

DON'T

DON'T tuck your napkin under your chin, or spread it upon your breast. Bibs and tuckers are for the nursery. Don't spread your napkin over your lap; let it fall over your knee.

Don't eat soup from the end of the spoon, but from the side. Don't gurgle, or draw in your breath, or make other noises when eating soup. Don't ask for a second service of soup.

Don't bite your bread. Break if off. Don't break your bread into your soup.

Don't use a steel knife with fish. A silver knife is now placed by the side of each plate for the fish course.

Don't eat vegetables with a spoon. Eat them with a fork. The rule is not to eat anything with a spoon that can be eaten with a fork. Even ices are now often eaten with a fork.

Don't leave your knife and fork on your plate when you send it for a second supply.

Don't apply to your neighbour to pass articles when the servant is at hand.

Don't, as guest, fold your napkin when you have finished. Place the napkin loosely on the table.

O. B. BUNCE ('CENSOR')
Don't: A Manual of Mistakes and Improprieties, 1883

I ALWAYS eat peas with honey,
  I've done it all my life:
They do taste kind of funny,
  But it keeps them on the knife.
ANONYMOUS

DR. SWIZZLE ON DIET

'You see, Sir Harry', he would say, 'it's all done by eating. More people dig their graves with their teeth than we imagine. Not that I would deny you the good things of this world, but I would recommend a few at a time, and no mixing. No side dishes. No liqueurs—only two or three wines. Whatever your stomach fancies, give it. Begin now, tomorrow, with the waters. A pint before breakfast—half an hour after, tea, fried ham, and eggs, brown bread, and a walk. Luncheon—another pint—a roast pigeon and fried potatoes, then a ride. Dinner at six, not later, mind; gravy soup, glass of sherry, nice fresh turbot and lobster sauce—wouldn't recommend salmon—another glass of sherry—then a good cut out of the middle of a well-browned saddle of mutton, wash it over with a few glasses of iced champagne; and if you like a little light pastry to wind up with, well and good. A pint of old port and a devilled biscuit can hurt no man. Mind, no salads, or cucumbers, or celery, at dinner, or fruit after. Turtle soup is very wholesome, so is venison. Don't let the punch be too acid though. Drink the water, live on a regimen, and you'll be well in no time.'

With these and suchlike comfortable assurances, he pocketed his guineas and bowed his patients out by the dozen.

ROBERT SMITH SURTEES
Handley Cross, 1842

TAVERN TALK

SOME men's whole delight is to take tobacco, and drink day long in a tavern or ale-house, to discourse, sing, all jest, roar, talk of a Cock and a Bull over a pot, &c.

ROBERT BURTON, *The Anatomy of Melancholy*, 1621

WOULD you know how we meet o'er our jolly full bowls?
As we mingle our liquors we mingle our souls:
The sweet melts the sharp, the kind soothes the strong,
And nothing but friendship grows all the night long.
     We drink, laugh, and gratify every desire
     Love only remains, our unquenchable fire.

THOMAS OTWAY, in *The Theatre of Music, II*, 1685

I HAVE heard him assert, that a tavern-chair was the throne of human felicity—'As soon', said he, 'as I enter the door of a tavern, I experience an oblivion of care, and a freedom from solicitude: when I am seated, I find the master courteous, and the servants obsequious to my call; anxious to know and ready to supply my wants: wine there exhilarates my spirits, and prompts me to free conversation and an interchange of discourse with those whom I most love: I dogmatize and am contradicted, and in this conflict of opinions and sentiments I find delight.'

SIR JOHN HAWKINS, *Life of Dr. Johnson*, 1787

FALSTAFF ON SHERRY

A GOOD sherris-sack hath a two-fold operation in it. It ascends me into the brain; dries me there all the foolish and dull and crudy vapours which environ it; makes it apprehensive, quick, forgetive, full of nimble, fiery and delectable shapes; which, delivered o'er to the voice, the tongue, which is the birth, becomes excellent wit. The second property of your excellent sherris is, the warming of the blood; which before, cold and settled, left the liver white and pale, which is the badge of pusillanimity and cowardice; but the sherris warms it and makes it course from the inwards to the parts extreme: it illumineth the face, which as a beacon gives warning to all the rest of this little kingdom, man, to arm; and then the vital commoners and inland petty spirits muster me all to their captain, the heart, who, great and puffed up with this retinue, doth any deed of courage; and this valour comes of sherris, so that skill in the weapon is nothing without sack, for that sets it a-work; and learning a mere hoard of gold kept by a devil, till sack commences it and sets it in act and use.

WILLIAM SHAKESPEARE
King Henry IV, Part II, 1600

KEATS ON CLARET

Now I like claret—Whenever I can have claret, I must drink it. 'Tis
the only palate affair that I am at all sensual in. Would it not be a
good speck to send you some vine-roots? Could it be done? I'll
enquire. If you could make some wine like claret, to drink on summer
evenings in an arbour! For really 'tis so fine. It fills one's mouth
with a gushing freshness, then goes down cool and feverless: then,
you do not feel it quarrelling with your liver. No; 'tis rather a peace-
maker, and lies as quiet as it did in the grape. Then it is as fragrant as
the Queen Bee, and the more ethereal part of it mounts into the
brain, not assaulting the cerebral apartments, like a bully in a bad
house looking for his trull, and hurrying from door to door, bounc-
ing against the wainscot, but rather walks like Aladdin about his
enchanted palace, so gently that you do not feel his step.

JOHN KEATS, Letter, Feb. 18, 1819

INDULGENCE

To unbosom my self frankly and freely to your Grace, I always looked upon drunkenness to be an unpardonable crime in a young fellow, who, without any of these foreign helps, has fire enough in his veins to enable him to do justice to Caelia whenever she demands a tribute from him. In a middle-age man, I consider the bottle as only subservient to the nobler pleasure of love; and he that would suffer himself to be so far infatuated by it, as to neglect the pursuit of a more agreeable game, I think deserves no quarter from the ladies. In old age indeed, when it is convenient to forget and steal from ourselves, I am of opinion that a little drunkenness, discreetly used, may as well contribute to our health of body as tranquillity of soul.

SIR GEORGE ETHEREGE, Letter to the
Duke of Buckingham, Nov. 12, 1686

His [Bishop Corbet's] chaplain, Dr. Lushington, was a very learned and ingenious man, and they loved one another. The bishop sometimes would take the key of the wine cellar, and he and his chaplain would go and lock themselves in and be merry. Then first he lays down his episcopal hat—'There lies the Doctor'. Then he puts off his gown—'There lies the Bishop'. Then 'twas: 'Here's to thee, Corbet!' and 'Here's to thee, Lushington!'

JOHN AUBREY, *Brief Lives* (written *c.* 1680)

A DOSE of salts has the effect of a temporary inebriation, like light champagne, on me.

GEORGE GORDON, LORD BYRON
Diary, January 6, 1821

84

BALLADE OF SOPORIFIC ABSORPTION

Ho! Ho! Yes! Yes! It's very all well,
    You may drunk I am think, but I tell you I'm not,
I'm as sound as a fiddle and fit as a bell,
    And stable quite ill to see what's what.
    I under *do* stand you surprise a got
When I headed my smear with gooseberry jam:
    And I've swallowed, I grant, a beer of lot—
But I'm not so think as you drunk I am.

Can I liquor my stand? Why, yes, like hell!
    I care not how many a tossed I've pot,
I shall stralk quite weight and not yutter an ell,
    My feech will not spalter the least little jot:
    If you knownly had own!—well, I gave him a dot,
And I said to him, 'Sergeant, I'll come like a lamb—
    The floor it seems like a storm in a yacht,
But I'm not so think as you drunk I am'.

For example, to prove it I'll tale you a tell—
    I once knew a fellow named Apricot—
I'm sorry, I just chair over a fell—
    A trifle—this chap, on a very day hot—
    If I hadn't consumed the last whisky of tot!—
As I said now, this fellow, called Abraham—
    Ah? One more? Since it's you! Just a do me will spot—
But I'm not so think as you drunk I am . . .

SIR JOHN SQUIRE
in *One Hundred & One Ballades*, 1931

VI: BEING AND DOING

CONSIDER the lilies of the field, how they grow; they toil not, neither do they spin: and yet I say unto you that even Solomon in all his glory was not arrayed like one of these.

THE GOSPEL ACCORDING TO ST. MATTHEW

A FOUNTAIN breaks out in the wilderness, but that fountain cares not whether any man comes to fetch water or no; a fresh and fit gale blows upon the sea, but it cares not whether the mariners hoist sail or no; a rose blows in your garden, but it calls you not to smell it.

JOHN DONNE, *Fifty Sermons*, 1649

BUSINESS is really more agreeable than pleasure; it interests the whole mind, the aggregate nature of man, more continuously, and more deeply. But it does not *look* as if it did.

WALTER BAGEHOT, *The English Constitution*, 1867

THOUGH the most be players, some must be spectators.

BEN JONSON, *Timber, or Discoveries made upon Men*, 1641

THE greater part of Men make their way with the same instinctiveness, the same unwandering eye from their purposes, the same animal eagerness as the Hawk . . . I go among the Fields and catch a glimpse of a Stoat or a fieldmouse peeping out of the withered grass—the creature hath a purpose, and its eyes are bright with it. I go amongst the buildings of a city and I see a Man hurrying along—to what? The Creature has a purpose, and his eyes are bright with it . . .

JOHN KEATS, Letter, 19 March, 1819

NOT he that knows how to acquire,
    But to enjoy, is blessed.
Nor does our happiness consist
    In motion, but in rest.

The gods pass man in bliss, because
    They toil not for more height,
But can enjoy, and in their own
    Eternal rest delight.

Then, princess, do not toil, nor care;
    Enjoy what you possess;
Which whilst you do, you equalize
    The gods in happiness.

THOMAS MAY
The Tragedy of Cleopatra, 1639
(acted 1626)

A CONFLICT

THERE were mornings when, casting off at dawn, I drifted through long cool shadows, watching the sunlight on the trees creep down to meet the water, hearing no sound but the tremolo of the aspens, seeing no one but a chance sportsman and his dog. There were noons with cooling breezes and flocculent clouds high in the sky, and evenings when the forest rang with bird song and the river was a sheet of moving glass. There were nights when, looking skywards, the passing clouds seemed like new continents and islands marked on the inside of a mighty globe.

Hereabouts there was just enough current to keep me moving through the stretches of restful, unexciting landscape. I could relax and let fancies flitter through my brain as inconsequentially as a ladybird or a drowsy moth might rest a moment on the gunwale.

The trouble with just 'being' is that you get nothing done. The trouble with 'doing' is that it makes you unconscious of 'being'. Nothing is worth doing unless you concentrate your thoughts upon it, yet if you do that you miss the consciousness of the doing, and enjoy only the having done.

ROBERT GIBBINGS
Coming Down the Seine, 1953

A SOLUTION

THE world contains so many beautiful things to gaze at
That gazing is an occupation that you could spend days at,
And these beautiful things are of so many different kinds, or shall
    we say heterogeneous,
Such as the sun and moon etc. and butterflies and mermaids etc.
    that to list them all you would have to be an etcetera genius,
So I shall hasten to a landing
And mention two beautiful things that are to my mind outstanding,
And one of them is to be on a train,
And see what we see when we flatten our noses against the pane,
And the other is wistful enough to make anybody feel cosmic and
    pious,
Which is to stand beside the track and wave at the passengers as they
    rocket by us,
So that is why rather than be an etcetera or any other kind of genius
I would rather be schizophrenious,
Because I should regard it as the most satisfactory of stunts
To be able to split my personality and be in two places at once,
For who could be so happy as I
Sitting with my nose against a train window watching me wave to
    me as I go rocketing by?

OGDEN NASH, 'Go Ahead, Look, and Listen'
Good Intentions, 1942

BUSYNESS AND IDLENESS

EXTREME busyness, whether at school or college, kirk or market, is a symptom of deficient vitality; and a faculty for idleness implies a catholic appetite and a strong sense of personal identity. There is a sort of dead-alive, hackneyed people about, who are scarcely conscious of living except in the exercise of some conventional occupation . . . they cannot be idle, their nature is not generous enough; and they pass those hours in a sort of coma, that are not dedicated to furious moiling in the gold-mill.

ROBERT LOUIS STEVENSON
Virginibus Puerisque, 1881

I LEAVE this notice on my door
For each accustomed visitor:
'I am gone into the fields
To take what this sweet hour yields;
Reflection, you may come tomorrow,
Sit by the fireside of Sorrow.
You with the unpaid bill, Despair,
You tiresome verse-reciter, Care,
I will pay you in the grave,
Death will listen to your stave.
Expectation too, be off!
Today is for itself enough . . .'

PERCY BYSSHE SHELLEY
Posthumous Poems, 1824

LYING AND LOOKING

A MARVELLOUSLY sweet occupation it is to lie on one's back in a wood and gaze upwards! You may fancy you are looking into a bottomless sea; that it stretches wide below you; that the trees are not rising out of the earth, but, like the roots of gigantic weeds, are dropping—falling straight down into those glassy, limpid depths; the leaves on the trees are at one moment transparent as emeralds, the next, they condense into golden, almost black green. Somewhere, afar off, at the end of a slender twig, a single leaf hangs motionless against the blue patch of transparent sky, and beside it another trembles with the motion of a fish on the line, as though moving of its own will, not shaken by the wind. Round white clouds float calmly across, and calmly pass away like submarine islands; and suddenly, all this ocean, this shining ether, these branches and leaves steeped in sunlight—all is rippling, quivering in fleeting brilliance, and a fresh trembling whisper awakens like the tiny, incessant plash of suddenly stirred eddies. One does not move—one looks, and no word can tell what peace, what joy, what sweetness reigns in the heart. One looks: the deep, pure blue stirs on one's lips a smile, innocent as itself; like the clouds over the sky, and, as it were, with them, happy memories pass in slow procession over the soul, and still one fancies one's gaze goes deeper and deeper, and draws one with it up into that peaceful, shining immensity, and that one cannot be brought back from that height, that depth.

IVAN TURGENEV, *A Sportsman's Sketches*, 1846
Translated by CONSTANCE GARNETT

CLIMBING

ELOQUENT are the hills: their power speaks
In ice, rock and falling stone;
The voices of croziered fern, wood-sorrel, gentian, edelweiss
Lead upward to the summit or the high col.

The mountain lake mirrors the hills, and the white clouds
Move in a blue depth, the hut stands empty:
No one appears all day, nothing disturbs
The symphony of ice and yellow rock and the blue shadow.

And at dusk the familiar sequence: the light
Lingering on the peak; and near the horizon
Apricot-coloured skies, then purple; and the first stars;
An hour of bustle in the hut, and then silence.

Only at two in the morning men stir in the bunks,
Look out of the windows, put on their boots,
Exchange a word with the guardian, curse the cold,
And move with a force beyond their own to the high peaks.

Be still for once. Do not sing,
Let the blood beat its symphony unanswered;
Remain here by the lake for a whole day
With the sky clear and the rocks asking to be climbed.

There is music in movement, in the song, the dance,
The swing of the accordion in the crowded hut,
The swing of the axe in the icefall; but be still.
Listen. There is another voice that speaks.

MICHAEL ROBERTS, 'The Green Lake'
Orion Marches, 1939

FLYING

I HELD the stick forward, nosing down and towards the road to counteract the drift of the wind. It was marvellous. I was aware, because of the nearness of the earth, of the roaring machine, headlong hurtling, racing over the surface of the earth. Sometimes I brought her really very low, and then as I saw trees looming up ahead, lifted her.

At Hilton, I did two turns round the house. I had no eyes for possible members of my family, but only for the elms as I roared off about twice their height.

With the wind behind us on the way back, we were going at the hell of a lick—about 120 miles an hour over the ground, so it was not long before hideous Girton heaved in view. I took her up a bit as I cut across to Chesterton. I shut off and brought her round perfectly to a good landing. 'Time for one more circuit.'

We took off all right, but over the elms the engine missed. Marshall throttled back, took over and lifted her up so steeply that I spoke my thought: 'What are you up to?'

He was gaining height for a conk out. Then he did a right-hand turn, shut the throttle and sang out: 'You've got her'.

I took her in and landed. I was drunk with air. I was wild and driving home sang and shouted, full of realization that we have found a new freedom—a new Ocean. For thousands of years we have crawled or run on the earth, or paddled across the seas, and all the while there has been this great ocean just over our heads in which at last we sail with joy. The longing for the sea: the call of the sea, one has heard of that, and that was the natural adventure in the past. But now it is a longing for the air, to go up. The air is more marvellous than any sea, it holds more beauty, more joy than any Pacific swell or South Sea lagoon.

DAVID GARNETT, *A Rabbit in the Air*, 1932

93

MINUET ON ICE

No motion can be more happily imagined for setting off an elegant figure to advantage; nor does the minuet itself afford half the opportunity of displaying a pretty foot. A lady may indulge herself here in a *tête à tête* with an acquaintance, without provoking the jealousy of her husband; and should she unfortunately make a slip, it would at least not be attended with any prejudice to her reputation.

The curved line on the outside edge . . . performed by a person of a genteel figure, is the most graceful and becoming movement of all others; and must appear to those who neither consider, nor understand, the reason of the body's being preserved so long in a falling position, as it were somewhat amazing: but, if mechanically considered, it may easily be conceived, with this allowance, that nature here, as well as on many occasions, acts in a manner that cannot be entirely reduced to mechanical principles.

ROBERT JONES
LIEUTENANT OF ARTILLERY
A Treatise on Skating, 1772

LA DAN
CRAY
DRAW
BY REN
I

DANSONS LA GIGUE!

DANSONS la gigue!

J'aimais surtout ses jolis yeux,
Plus clairs que l'étoile des cieux,
J'aimais ses yeux malicieux.

Dansons la gigue!

Elle avait des façons vraiment
De désoler un pauvre amant,
Que c'en était vraiment charmant.

Dansons la gigue!

Mais je trouve encore meilleur
Le baiser de sa bouche en fleur,
Depuis qu'elle est morte à mon coeur.

Dansons la gigue!

Je me souviens, je me souviens
Des heures et des entretiens,
Et c'est le meilleur de mes biens.

Dansons la gigue!

PAUL VERLAINE, 'Streets'
Romances sans Paroles, 1874

WALKING AT NIGHT

By sundown we had made some distance, even by our slow rate of progress, though to be sure the sentry on the rock was still plainly in our view. But now we came on something that put all fears out of season; and that was a deep rushing burn, that tore down, in that part, to join the glen river. At the sight of this we cast ourselves on the ground and plunged head and shoulders in the water; and I cannot tell which was the more pleasant, the great shock as the cool stream went over us, or the greed with which we drank of it.

We lay there (for the banks hid us), drank again and again, bathed our chests, let our wrists trail in the running water till they ached with the chill; and at last, being wonderfully renewed, we got out the meal-bag and made drammach in the iron pan. . . .

As soon as the shadow of the night had fallen, we set forth again, at first with the same caution, but presently with more boldness, standing our full height and stepping out at a good pace of walking. The way was very intricate, lying up the steep sides of mountains and along the brows of cliffs; clouds had come in with the sunset, and the night was dark and cool; so that I walked without much fatigue, but in continual fear of falling and rolling down the mountains, and with no guess at our direction.

The moon rose at last and found us still on the road; it was in its last quarter, and was long beset with clouds; but after a while shone out and showed me many dark heads of mountains, and was reflected far underneath us on the narrow arm of a sea-loch.

At this sight we both paused; I struck with wonder to find myself so high and walking (as it seemed to me) upon clouds . . .

ROBERT LOUIS STEVENSON, *Kidnapped*, 1886

SITTING AND LOOKING

I KNOW nothing so pleasant as to sit there on a summer afternoon, with the western sun flickering through the great elder-tree, and lighting up our gay parterres, where flowers and flowering shrubs are set as thick as grass in a field, a wilderness of blossoms, interwoven, intertwined, wreathy, garlandy, profuse beyond all profusion, where we may guess that there is such a thing as mould, but never see it. I know nothing so pleasant as to sit in the shade of that dark bower, with the eye resting on that bright piece of colour, lighted so gloriously by the evening sun, now catching a glimpse of the little birds as they fly rapidly in and out of their nests—for there are always two or more birds'-nests in the thick tapestry of cherry-trees, honeysuckle, and china-roses which covers our walls—now tracing the gay symbols of the common butterflies, as they sport around the dahlias; now watching that rarer moth, which the country people, fertile in pretty names, call the bee-bird; that bird-like insect which flutters in the hottest days over the sweetest flowers, inserting its long proboscis into the small tube of the jessamine, and hovering over the scarlet blossoms of the geranium, whose bright colour seems reflected on its own feathery breast; that insect, which seems so thoroughly a creature of the air, never at rest; always, even when feeding, self-poised and self-supported, and whose wings, in their ceaseless motion, have a sound so deep, so full, so lulling, so musical.

Nothing so pleasant as to sit amid that mixture of the flower and the leaf, watching the bee-bird! Nothing so pretty to look at as my garden! It is quite a picture; only unluckily it resembles a picture in more qualities than one,—it is fit for nothing but to look at.

MARY RUSSELL MITFORD, *Our Village*, vol. 3, 1828

TO SEA! TO SEA!

To sea! To sea! The calm is o'er,
The wanton water leaps in sport,
And rattles down the pebbly shore;
The dolphin wheels, the sea-cows snort,
And unseen Mermaids' pearly song
Comes bubbling up, the weeds among.
  Fling broad the sail, dip deep the oar:
  To sea! To sea! The calm is o'er.

To sea! To sea! Our wide-winged bark
Shall billowy cleave its sunny way,
And with its shadow, fleet and dark,
Break the caved Triton's azure ray,
Like mighty eagle soaring light
O'er antelopes on Alpine height.
  The anchor heaves, the ship swings free,
  The sails swell full: To sea, to sea!

THOMAS LOVELL BEDDOES
Death's Jest-Book, 1850

SCHOONER UNDER A MOON: PAINTING BY ALFRED WALLIS, *c.* 1936

A CARP
IN A POOL:
COLOURED
WOODCUT BY
KATSUSHIKA TAITO
(NINETEENTH
CENTURY)

DARK ECSTACIES

In a cool curving world he lies
And ripples with dark ecstasies.
The kind luxurious lapse and steal
Shapes all his universe to feel
And know and be; the clinging stream
Closes his memory, glooms his dream,
Who lips the roots o' the shore, and glides
Superb on unreturning tides.
Those silent waters weave for him
A fluctuant mutable world and dim,
Where wavering masses bulge and gape
Mysterious, and shape to shape
Dies momently through whorl and hollow,
And form and line and solid follow
Solid and line and form to dream
Fantastic down the eternal stream;
An obscure world, a shifting world,
Bulbous, or pulled to thin, or curled,
Or serpentine, or driving arrows,
Or serene slidings, or March narrows.
There slipping wave and shore are one,
And weed and mud. No ray of sun,
But glow to glow fades down the deep
(As dream to unknown dream in sleep);
Shaken translucency illumes
The hyaline of drifting glooms . . .

RUPERT BROOKE, from 'The Fish'
Poems, 1911

OH ! THE WILD JOYS OF LIVING !

OH ! the wild joys of living ! the leaping from rock up to rock—
The strong rending of boughs from the fir-tree—the cool silver shock
Of the plunge in a pool's living water,—the hunt of the bear,
And the sultriness showing the lion is couched in his lair.
And the meal—the rich dates yellowed over with gold dust divine,
And the locust's flesh steeped in the pitcher ! the full draught of wine,
And the sleep in the dried river-channel where bulrushes tell
That the water was wont to go warbling so softly and well.
How good is man's life, the mere living ! how fit to employ
All the heart and the soul and the senses, for ever in joy !

ROBERT BROWNING, 'Saul'
Men and Women, 1855

Mrs. Sullen: Country pleasures ! Racks and torments ! Dost think,
child, that *my* limbs were made for leaping of ditches and clambering
over stiles?

GEORGE FARQUHAR, *The Beaux' Stratagem*, 1706

THE ELEGANT LIFE

LET us push the swing-door of Maxim's to-night and pass through into this bright, new world of elegance, of gaiety, of *entrain* and abandon in evening clothes. A brilliant and fascinating sight meets the eye. Behind and in front of little tables spread with the finest napery, men and women, representing the last word in fashion, are discussing supper. The gilded necks of champagne-bottles emerge, at a comfortable and convivial angle, from ice-pails, and plates are occupied with the solid vestiges of succulent *ostendes* and *marennes vertes*. The theatres and music-halls, the Opera and the concerts, have disgorged their world, and it comes here to while away an hour on feathery wings before departing homewards in swift Panhard or *voiture de maitre* . . . Parisian gaiety bubbles and froths like champagne every night in the year. The best-dressed, wittiest, and prettiest women of the *monde* are supping here with their male friends and relatives, who are sure to be some of the smartest men in diplomacy and the world of affairs.

As the night proceeds in the *chaleur communicative de banquet*—to quote a phrase which had its vogue in Paris and its political allusion—the music of the red-coated band becomes more exhilarating and more alluring. It intoxicates the brain, it invades the feet; it invites to the waltz. And presently there are couples swaying rhythmically, with swishing feet, upon the floor. Some professional beauty, with glittering eyes and marble throat, embellished with costly pearls, is waltzing divinely in the arms of an American king of postage stamps. It is an enchanting scene,—this light-hearted, swift, and evanescent fun, which never degenerates into vulgarity and never goes beyond the borders set by discretion and good taste.

The Illustrated London News, 1907

FOIBLES

LORD BUTE, when young, possessed a very handsome person, of which advantage he was not insensible; and he used to pass many hours every day, as his enemies asserted, occupied in contemplating the symmetry of his own legs.

SIR NATHANIEL WRAXALL, *Historical Memoirs*, 1836

'IF (said he) I had no duties, and no reference to futurity, I would spend my life in driving briskly in a post-chaise with a pretty woman; but she should be one who could understand me, and would add something to the conversation.'

JAMES BOSWELL, *Life of Dr. Johnson*, 1791

. . . OVER Lamb, at this period of his life, there passed regularly, after taking wine, a brief eclipse of sleep. It descended upon him as softly as a shadow. In a gross person, laden with superfluous flesh, and sleeping heavily, this would have been disagreeable; but in Lamb, thin even to meagreness, spare and wiry as an Arab of the desert, or as Thomas Aquinas, wasted by scholastic vigils, the affection of sleep seemed rather a network of aerial gossamer than of earthly cobweb—more like a golden haze falling upon him gently from the heavens than a cloud exhaling upwards from the flesh. Motionless in his chair as a bust, breathing so gently as scarcely to seem certainly alive, he presented the image of repose midway between life and death, like the repose of sculpture; and, to one who knew his history, a repose affectingly contrasting with the calamities and internal storms of his life.

THOMAS DE QUINCEY, *Leaders in Literature*, 1858

MORE FOIBLES

I MENTIONED that Lord Monboddo told me he awaked every morning at four, and then for his health got up and walked in his room naked, with the window open, which he called taking an air bath; after which he went to bed again, and slept two hours more.

JAMES BOSWELL, *Life of Dr. Johnson*, 1791

AT night, when he was abed, and the doors made fast, and was sure nobody heard him, he sang aloud (not that he had a very good voice) but for his health's sake: he did believe it did his lungs good, and conduced much to prolong his life.

JOHN AUBREY
on Thomas Hobbes, *Brief Lives*, (written *c.* 1680)

I LOVE in Isa's bed to lie
O such a joy and luxury
The bottom of the bed I sleep
And with great care I myself keep
Oft I embrace her feet of lillys
But she has goton all the pillies
Her neck I never can embrace
But I do hug her feet in place.

MARJORIE FLEMING, aged seven, quoted by
DR. JOHN BROWN, *Horae Subsecivae*, 1858

NIGHTS OUT

SIR, there is nothing which has yet been contrived by man by which so much happiness is produced as by a good tavern or inn.

SAMUEL JOHNSON, in Boswell's *Life*, 1791

AFTER that I played on my flageolet, and stayed there till nine o'clock, very merry and drawn on with one song after another till it came to be so late. After that Sheply, Harrison and myself, we went towards Westminster on foot, and at the Golden Lion, near Charing Cross, we went in and drank a pint of wine, and so parted, and thence home, where I found my wife and maid a-washing. I sat up till the bell-man came by with his bell just under my window as I was writing of this very line, and cried, 'Past one of the clock, and a cold, frosty, windy morning'. I then went to bed, and left my wife and the maid a-washing still.

SAMUEL PEPYS, *Diary*, 16 January, 1660

THE servant gave me my coat and hat, and in a glow of self-satisfaction I walked out into the night. 'A delightful evening,' I reflected, 'the nicest kind of people. What I said about finance and philosophy impressed them; and how they laughed when I imitated a pig squealing.'

But soon after, 'God, it's awful', I muttered, 'I wish I was dead'.

LOGAN PEARSALL SMITH, *Trivia*, 1918

ODD MAN OUT

WHEN I'm among a blaze of lights,
With tawdry music and cigars
And women dawdling through delights,
And officers in cocktail bars,
Sometimes I think of garden nights
And elm trees nodding at the stars.

I dream of a small firelit room
With yellow candles burning straight,
And glowing pictures in the gloom,
And kindly books that hold me late.
Of things like these I choose to think
When I can never be alone:
Then someone says 'Another drink?'
And turns my living heart to stone.

SIEGFRIED SASSOON
The Old Huntsman, and Other Poems, 1917

EXPRESS GALOP

... PASS through the arch; put your ear to the ground!
This road sweepeth on through the isle and around!
You touch that which touches the country's bound!
                        'Tis the railroad!
Like arrowy lightning snatch'd from the sky,
And bound to the earth, the bright rails lie;
And their way is straight driven through mountains high,
And headland to headland o'er valleys they tie;
                        'Tis the railroad!

See how the engine hums still on the rails,
While his long train of cars slowly down to him sails;
He staggers like a brain blooded high, and he wails;
                        'Tis the railroad!
His irons take the cars, and screaming he goes;
Now may heaven warn before him all friends and all foes!
A whole city's missives within him repose,
Half a thousand miles his, ere the day's hours close;
                        'Tis the railroad!

EBENEZER JONES
Studies of Sensation and Event, 1843

THE EXPRESS GALOP: LITHOGRAPH BY JOHN BRANDARD, *c.* 1850

JOCKEYS: PAINTING BY RAOUL DUFY, 1945

LOOK AT THAT HORSE!

LOOK at that horse! Must such a beauty die
To let more motor-bicycles rush by?
Go to your Parliament and search the crowd
For brows as thoughtful and an eye so proud!
Alas, we cannot with a dealer's art
Pick out his points and duly praise each part
(We know the horse as little as the car
And are not certain what the withers are),
But he indeed must have a flint for soul
Who without reverence regards the whole.
What fairy step!—that drop of Arab blood,
Sahara's tribute to the English stud!
Brave as a lion and as hard to kill,
He can stand anything but standing still.
He is on wires, suspended from the skies,
He is elastic—it would not surprise
If on a sudden he took wings and *flew*
Over the Downs and off to Timbuktu.
You are in love with your new petrol-pump,
But there's more splendour in the creature's *rump*!
No wonder, then your Marquis bows his head
When he confronts an English thoroughbred!
See what a wise unwinking pair they stand,
The last patricians in a vulgar land,
While milord murmurs in the mobile ear
'We are back numbers, you and I, my dear'.
And the brave beast would whisper if he could:
'We may be going, but by God, we're good!'

SIR ALAN HERBERT, *Derby Day*, 1931

VII: LOVING

United souls are not satisfied with embraces, but desire to be truly each other; which being impossible, their desires are infinite, and proceed without a possibility of satisfaction. Another misery there is in affection, that whom we truly love like our own selves, we forget their looks, nor can our memory retain the Idea of their faces; and it is no wonder, for they are our selves, and our affection makes their looks our own.

SIR THOMAS BROWNE, *Religio Medici*, 1643

Perfect love has this advantage in it, that it leaves the possessor of it nothing farther to desire. There is one object (at least) in which the soul finds absolute content, for which it seeks to live, or dares to die. The heart has, as it were, filled up the moulds of the imagination. The truth of passion keeps pace with and outvies the extravagance of mere language. There are no words so fine, no flattery so soft, that there is not a sentiment beyond them, that it is impossible to express, at the bottom of the heart where true love is.

WILLIAM HAZLITT, *Liber Amoris*, 1823

COME hither, you that love, and hear me sing
    Of joys still growing,
Green, fresh, and lusty as the pride of spring,
    And ever blowing.
Come hither, youths that blush, and dare not know
    What is desire:
And old men, worse than you, that cannot blow
    One spark of fire;
And with the power of my enchanting song,
Boys shall be able men, and old men young.

Come hither, you that hope, and you that cry;
    Leave off complaining;
Youth, strength, and beauty, that shall never die,
    Are here remaining.
Come hither, fools, and blush you stay so long
    From being blest;
And mad men, worse than you, that suffer wrong,
    Yet seek no rest;
And in an hour, with my enchanting song,
You shall be ever pleased, and young maids long.

JOHN FLETCHER, *The Captain*, 1647

WINGS FOR PHANTASY

LOVE, sweet Chloe, is a god, a young youth, and very fair, and winged to fly. And therefore he delights in youth, follows beauty, and gives our phantasy her wings. His power's so vast that that of Jove is not so great. He governs in the elements, rules in the stars, and domineers even o'er the gods that are his peers . . . All flowers are the works of Love. Those plants are his creations, and poems. By him it is that the rivers flow, and by him the winds blow. I have known a bull that has been in love and run bellowing through the meadows as if he had been pricked with a goad; a he-goat, too, so in love with a virgin-she that he has followed her up and down, through the woods, through the lawns. And I myself, when I was young, was in love with Amaryllis, and forgot to eat my meat and drink my drink, and for many tedious nights never could compose to sleep. My panting heart was very sad and anxious, and my body shook with cold: I cried out oft as if I had been thwacked and basted back and sides: and then again was still and mute as if I had lain among the dead. I cast myself into the rivers, as if I had been all on a fire: I called on Pan that he would help me, as having sometimes been himself catched with the love of the peevish Pities. I praised the Echo, that with kindness it restored and trebled to me the dear name of Amaryllis. I broke my pipes, because they could delight, and led the sturdy herds which way I would, and could not draw the forward girl. For there is no medicine for love, neither meat, nor drink, nor any charm, but only kissing and embracing, and lying naked together.

LONGUS, *Daphnis and Chloe*
translated by George Thorneley, 1657

POET IN THE CHARACTER OF A SHEPHERD: PAINTING BY SIR PETER LELY, *c.* 1645

THE HON.
MRS GRAHA
PAINTING
BY THOMAS
GAINSBORO
R.A.
1777

WOMAN

I CONSIDER woman as a beautiful romantic animal, that may be adorned with furs and feathers, pearls and diamonds, ores and silks. The lynx shall cast its skin at her feet to make her a tippet; the peacock, parrot and swan shall pay contributions to her muff; the sea shall be searched for shells, and the rocks for gems; and every part of nature furnish out its share towards the embellishment of a creature that is the most consummate work of it.

JOSEPH ADDISON, in *The Tatler*, No. 116, 1711

WOMAN (doubtful theme) I sing,
Dear, delightful, dangerous thing!
Magic source of all our joy,
Tempting, trifling, tinselled toy:
Every faculty possessing
That constitutes a curse or blessing:
Witty, empty, fond, capricious,
Pious sometimes, often vicious:
As angels handsome, devils proud,
Modest, pert, submissive, loud:
The most ambiguous work of Heaven,
To cheer us, and torment us, given:
Without them, what, ye gods, is life?
And with them—what but care and strife?

ANONYMOUS, in
A Collection of English Songs, 1796

MAN

My beloved is white and ruddy, the chiefest among ten thousand.
His head is as the most fine gold, his locks are bushy and black as a
raven. His eyes are as the eyes of doves by the rivers of waters,
washed with milk and fitly set. His cheeks are as a bed of spices, as
sweet flowers: his lips like lilies dropping sweet-smelling myrrh.
His hands are as gold rings set with the beryl: his belly is as bright
ivory overlaid with sapphires. His legs are as pillars of marble set
upon sockets of fine gold; his countenance is as Lebanon, excellent
as the cedars. His mouth is most sweet; yea, he is altogether lovely.

Solomon's Song, 10

Lo! in the palace, lo! in the street,
    Beautiful beyond measure;
Yea, gods for glory, and women for sweet,
    The youths, the princes of pleasure!

Idle and crowned in the long day's sun,
    Turbulent, passionate, sad;
Full of the soul of the deed to be done,
    Or the thought of the joy latest had;
They walk their way through the crowds that run,
    They pass through the crowds that part;
And the women behold them, and each knows one,
    How mighty he is in her heart . . .

They win with the vehemence of their souls,
    With the swiftness of their fame;
Their strong and radiant look controls,
    And smiles the world to shame.
Their rule is large, and like fair lords,
    They lavish a goodly treasure;
They live of the joy the world affords
    And they pay the world with pleasure.

One passes bright through the street down there,
    Named and known of repute;
And one hath a scandal of rich flowing hair,
    And the musical tongue of a lute.
O the women, beholding, who thrill and say,
    'While that one stays on the earth,
I can have in the secret of night or of day,
    More delight than a man's life is worth'.

O the woman that says in the midst of the crowd,
    'Beautiful, turbulent one,
Do I not know you through semblance and shroud,
    Even as I know the sun?
Burning, and swift, and divine you are;
    But I have you all to treasure;
Women may love you, but mine you are,
    And prince of the princes of pleasure.'

ARTHUR O'SHAUGHNESSY, from 'A Song of
the Youths', *Music and Moonlight*, 1874

THE NATURE OF LOVE

THAT violence wherewith sometimes a man doteth upon one creature is but a little spark of that love, even towards all, which lurketh in his nature. We are made to love, both to satisfy the necessity of our active nature, and to answer the beauties in every creature. By love our souls are married and solder'd to the creatures: and it is our duty like God to be united to them all. We must love them infinitely, but in God, and for God: and God in them: namely all His excellencies manifested in them. When we dote upon the perfections and beauties of some one creature, we do not love that too much, but other things too little. Never was anything in this world loved too much, but many things have been loved in a false way: and all in too short a measure.

THOMAS TRAHERNE, *Centuries of Meditations*, 1908
(written *c.* 1670)

WHAT thing is love? for sure love is a thing.
It is a prick, it is a sting,
It is a pretty, pretty thing;
It is a fire, it is a coal,
Whose flame creeps in at every hole;
And, as my wit doth best devise,
Love's dwelling is in ladies' eyes,
From whence do glance love's piercing darts
That make such holes into our hearts . . .

GEORGE PEELE
The Hunting of Cupid, 1591

FIRST LOVE

WHEN I was in my fourteenth year,
And captain of the third eleven,
I fell in love with Guenevere,
And hovered at the gate of heaven.
She wasn't more than twenty-seven.

I partnered her, by happy chance,
At tennis, losing every game.
No shadow dimmed her careless glance,
No teasing word, no hint of blame.
Brightlier burned my secret flame.

Nothing I asked but to adore,
In dumb surrender, shy and stiff:
But ah, she gave me how much more,
A benison beyond belief!
'Just hold my racquet for a jiff.'

GERALD BULLETT
Windows on a Vanished Time, 1955

IN LOVE

ONCE did my thoughts both ebb and flow,
  As passion did them move;
Once did I hope, straight fear again—
  And then I was in love.

Once did I waking spend the night,
  And tell how many minutes move;
Once did I wishing waste the day—
  And then I was in love.

Once, by my carving true love's knots,
  The weeping trees did prove
That wounds and tears were both our lots—
  And then I was in love.

Once did I breathe another's breath
  And in my mistress move;
Once was I not mine own at all—
  And then I was in love . . .

Once did I sonnet to my saint,
  My soul in number moved,
Once did I tell a thousand lies—
  And then in truth I loved.

Once in my ear did dangling hang
  A little turtle-dove,
Once, in a word, I was a fool—
  And then I was in love.

ANONYMOUS, set to music by Robert Jones
in *The Muse's Garden for Delights*, 1610

THE MOOD OF MAY

WHEN May is in his prime, then may each heart rejoice:
When May bedecks each branch with green, each bird strains forth
  his voice.
The lively sap creeps up into the blooming thorn;
The flowers, which cold in prison kept, now laugh the frost to scorn.
All nature's imps triùmph whiles joyful May doth last;
When May is gone, of all the year the pleasant time is past.

May makes the cheerful hue, May breeds and brings new blood;
May marcheth throughout every limb, May makes the merry mood.
May pricketh tender hearts their warbling notes to tune:
Full strange it is, yet some we see do make their May in June.
Thus things are strangely wrought whiles joyful May doth last,
Take May in time, when May is gone the pleasant time is past.

All ye that live on earth, and have your May at will,
Rejoice in May, as I do now, and use your May with skill.
Use May while that you may, for May hath but his time,
When all the fruit is gone, it is too late the tree to climb.
Your liking and your lust is fresh whiles May doth last;
When May is gone, of all the year the pleasant time is past.

RICHARD EDWARDS
The Paradise of Dainty Devices, 1576

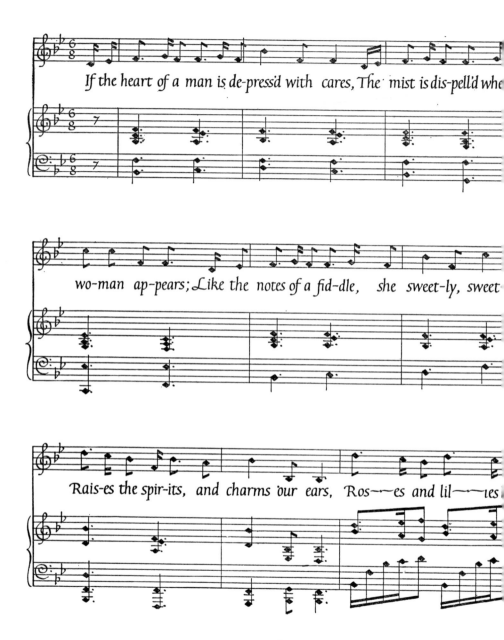

If the heart of a man is de-press'd with cares, The mist is dis-pell'd whe

wo-man ap-pears; Like the notes of a fid-dle, she sweet-ly, sweet

Rais-es the spir-its, and charms our ears, Ros——es and lil——ies

cheeks · dis–close,　　But her ripe lips are more sweet than those.

Press her, Ca-ress her, With blisses, Her kisses Dis-solve us in pleasure and soft re-pose.

TRADITIONAL　　　　WORDS BY JOHN GAY, *The Beggar's Opera,* 1728

QUESTIONS

WHEN wert thou born, Desire?
  In pride and pomp of May.
By whom, sweet boy, wert thou begot?
  By Self Conceit, men say.
Tell me, who was thy nurse?
  Fresh Youth in sugared joy.
What was thy meat and daily food?
  Sad sighs and great annoy.
What hadst thou then to drink?
  Unfeignëd lovers' tears.
What cradle wert thou rocked in?
  In hope devoid of fears.
What brought thee to thy sleep?
  Sweet thoughts, which liked me best.
And where is now thy dwelling-place?
  In gentle hearts I rest.
Doth company displease?
  It doth, in many one.
Where would Desire then choose to be?
  He loves to muse alone.
What feedeth most thy sight?
  To gaze on favour still.
Whom find'st thou most thy foe?
  Disdain of my good will.
Will ever age or death
  Bring thee unto decay?
No, no! Desire both lives and dies
  A thousand times a day.

EDWARD DE VERE, EARL OF OXFORD, Bodley MS.

AND ANSWERS

Ask me no more where Jove bestows,
When June is past, the fading rose;
For in your beauties, orient deep,
These flowers, as in their causes, sleep.

Ask me no more whither do stray
The golden atoms of the day;
For in pure love heaven did prepare
Those powders to enrich your hair.

Ask me no more whither doth haste
The nightingale, when May is past;
For in your sweet dividing throat
She winters, and keeps warm her note.

Ask me no more where those stars light
That downwards fall in dead of night;
For in your eyes they sit, and there
Fixèd become, as in their sphere.

Ask me no more if east or west
The phoenix builds her spicy nest;
For unto you at last she flies,
And in your fragrant bosom dies.

THOMAS CAREW, *Poems*, 1640

THE WINGED CHARIOT

HAD we but world enough, and time,
This coyness, lady, were no crime,
We would sit down, and think which way
To walk, and pass our long love's day.
Thou by the Indian Ganges' side
Shouldst rubies find: I by the tide
Of Humber would complain. I would
Love you ten years before the flood,
And you should, if you please, refuse
Till the conversion of the Jews;
My vegetable love should grow
Vaster than empires and more slow;
An hundred years should go to praise
Thine eyes, and on thy forehead gaze;
Two hundred to adore each breast,
But thirty thousand to the rest;
An age at least to every part,
And the last age should show your heart.
For, lady, you deserve this state,
Nor would I love at lower rate,
  But at my back I always hear
Time's wingèd chariot hurrying near,
And yonder all before us lie
Deserts of vast eternity . . .

ANDREW MARVELL, *Miscellaneous Poems*, 1684
(written before 1653)

GATHER YE ROSE-BUDS

GATHER ye rose-buds while ye may,
   Old Time is still a-flying:
And this same flower that smiles today,
   Tomorrow will be dying.

The glorious lamp of heaven, the sun
   The higher he's a-getting,
The sooner will his race be run,
   And nearer he's to setting.

That age is best which is the first,
   When youth and blood are warmer;
But being spent, the worse, and worst
   Times still succeed the former.

Then be not coy, but use your time;
   And while ye may, go marry:
For having lost but once your prime,
   You may for ever tarry.

ROBERT HERRICK, *Hesperides*, 1648

THE FOUNTAINS SMOKE

THE fountains smoke, and yet no flames they show;
  Stars shine all night, though undiscerned by day;
And trees do spring, yet are not seen to grow;
  And shadows move, although they seem to stay.
    In winter's woe is buried summer's bliss,
    And Love loves most when Love most secret is.

The stillest streams descry the greatest deep;
  The clearest sky is subject to a shower;
Conceit's most sweet whenas it seems to sleep;
  And fairest days do in the morning lower.
    The silent groves sweet nymphs they cannot miss,
    For Love loves most where Love most secret is.

The rarest jewels hidden virtue yield;
  The sweet of traffic is a secret gain;
The year once old doth show a barren field;
  And plants seem dead, and yet they spring again:
    Cupid is blind: the reason why is this:
    Love loveth most when Love most secret is.

ANONYMOUS, set to music by Robert Jones in
The Muse's Garden for Delights, 1610

DEATH OF A HERO

WHAT shall I do to show how much I love her?
 How many millions of sighs can suffice?
That which wins other hearts, never can move her,
 Those common methods of love she'll despise.

I will love more than man e'er loved before me,
 Gaze on her all the day, melt all the night,
Till for her own sake at last she'll implore me
 To love her less, to preserve our delight.

Since gods themselves could not ever be loving,
 Men must have breathing recruits for new joys;
I wish my love could be always improving,
 Though eager love, more than sorrow, destroys.

In fair Aurelia's arms leave me expiring
 To be embalmed by the sweets of her breath,
To the last moment I'll still be desiring:
 Never had hero so glorious a death.

THOMAS BETTERTON, *The Prophetess*, 1690

GOLDEN FETTERS

WHILST I behold thy glittering golden hairs
Dishevelled thus, waving about thy ears,
And see those locks thus loosëd and undone
For their more pomp to sport them in the sun,
Love takes those threads and weaves them with that art
He knits a thousand knots about my heart,
And with such skill and cunning he them sets,
My soul lies taken in those lovely nets,
Making me cry, 'Fair prison, that dost hold
My heart in fetters wrought of burnished gold.'

JAMES MABBE, *Exemplary Novels*, 1640

CHOOSING:
PAINTING OF ELLEN TERRY
BY G. F. WATTS, R.A., 1864

THE BATHERS: PAINTING BY WILLIAM MULREADY, R.A., 1849

BEHOLD!

HAVE you a desire to see
The glorious heaven's epitome?
Or an abstract of the Spring?
Adonis' garden? or a thing
    Fuller of wonder, Nature's shop displayed
    Hung with the choicest pieces she has made?
    Here behold it open laid.

Or else would you bless your eyes
With a type of paradise?
Or behold how poets feign
Jove to sit amidst his train?
    Or see (what made Actaeon rue)
    Diana 'mongst her virgin crew?
    Lift up your eyes and view.

PETER HAUSTED
The Rival Friends, 1632

LOVE LINE

My love is of a birth as rare
    As 'tis for object strange and high:
It was begotten by Despair
    Upon Impossibility.

Magnanimous Despair alone
    Could show me so divine a thing,
Where feeble Hope could ne'er have flown
    But vainly flapped its tinsel wing . . .

Unless the giddy heaven fall,
    And earth some new convulsion tear,
And, us to join, the world should all
    Be cramped into a planisphere.

As lines, so loves oblique may well
    Themselves in every angle greet:
But ours, so truly parallel,
    Though infinite can never meet.

Therefore the love which us doth bind,
    But Fate so enviously debars,
Is the conjunction of the mind,
    And opposition of the stars.

ANDREW MARVELL
Miscellaneous Poems, 1681
(written about 1650)

EXPRESSION

I AM two fools, I know,
For loving, and for saying so
   In whining poetry;
But where's that wise man that would not be I,
   If she would not deny?
Then as th' earth's inward narrow crooked lanes
Do purge sea-water's fretful salt away,
   I thought, if I could draw my pains
Through rhyme's vexation, I should them allay.
Grief brought to numbers cannot be so fierce,
For he tames it, that fetters it in verse.

   But when I have done so,
Some man, his art and voice to show,
   Doth set and sing my pain,
And, by delighting many, frees again
   Grief, which verse did restrain.
To Love and Grief tribute of Verse belongs,
But not of such as pleases when tis' read;
   Both are increasèd by such songs:
For both their triumphs so are publishèd,
And I, which was two fools, do so grow three;
Who are a little wise, the best fools be.

JOHN DONNE, *Poems*, 1633
(written *c.* 1598)

KISSING HER HAIR

KISSING her hair I sat against her feet,
Wove and unwove it, wound and found it sweet;
Made fast therewith her hands, drew down her eyes,
Deep as deep flowers and dreamy like dim skies;
With her own tresses bound and found her fair,
     Kissing her hair.

Sleep were no sweeter than her face to me,
Sleep of cold sea-bloom under the cold sea;
What pain could get between my face and hers?
What new sweet thing would love not relish worse?
Unless, perhaps, white death had kissed me there,
     Kissing her hair?

ALGERNON CHARLES SWINBURNE
'Rondel', *Poems and Ballads*, 1866

MIRRORS OF LOVE

DEAR, let us two each other spy:
How curious! In each other's eye
We're drawn to life, and thus we see
Ourselves at once, both thee and me,
Distinctly two, yet not alone,
Incorporated, that's but one.

My picture in your eyes you bear:
I yours, as much as mine you wear.
'Tis not our speties can not pass,
Or shining makes a looking glass,
Nor picture, really we lie
Contracted each in other's eye.

When that our milk-white purer lawn,
Our eyelid curtains, when they're drawn,
Soft sleep, made with sweet vapour's rain,
To cool us shrinks into each brain,
Rejoicing with love's running streams,
Which grosser lovers call but dreams.

Because we two must never part,
We move down to each other's heart,
And there, all passions turned to joy,
Our loving hearts feel no annoy
Delated, lest our souls outskips
With joy, kiss quickly! stop our lips!

WILLIAM CAVENDISH, DUKE OF NEWCASTLE
The Phanseys, c. 1645

THE MEANING OF A KISS

... ALTHOUGH the mouth be a parcel of the body, yet is it an issue for the words, that be the interpreters of the soul, and for the inward breath, which is also called the soul. And therefore hath a delight to join his mouth with a woman's beloved with a kiss: not to stir him to any dishonest desire, but because he feeleth that that bond is the opening of an entry to the souls, which, drawn with a coveting the one of the other, pour themselves by turn the one into the other body, and be so mingled together that each of them hath two souls.

BALDASSARE CASTIGLIONE, *The Courtier*
translated by Sir Thomas Hoby, 1561

ALL the breath and the bloom of the year in the bag of one bee:
All the wonder and wealth of the mine in the heart of one gem:
In the core of one pearl all the shade and the shine of the sea:
Breath and bloom, shade and shine,—wonder, wealth, and—how far
   above them—
     Truth, that's brighter than gem,
     Trust, that's purer than pearl—
Brightest truth, purest trust in the universe—
     All were for me in the kiss of one girl.

ROBERT BROWNING, 'Summer Bonum', *Asolando*, 1889

ARITHMETIC OF THE LIPS

GIVE me a kiss from those sweet lips of thine
And make it double by enjoining mine,
Another yet, nay yet and yet another,
And let the first kiss be the second's brother.
Give me a thousand kisses and yet more;
And then repeat those that have gone before;
Let us begin while daylight springs in heaven,
And kiss till night descends into the even,
And when that modest secretary, night,
Discolours all but thy heaven beaming bright,
We will begin revels of hidden love
In that sweet orb where silent pleasures move.
In high new strains, unspeakable delight,
We'll vent the dull hours of the silent night:
Were the bright day no more to visit us,
Oh, then for ever would I hold thee thus,
Naked, enchained, empty of idle fear,
As the first lovers in the garden were.
I'll die betwixt thy breasts that are so white,
For, to die there, would do a man delight.
Embrace me still, for time runs on before,
And being dead we shall embrace no more.
Let us kiss faster than the hours do fly,
Long live each kiss and never know to die . . .
Let us vie kisses, till our eyelids cover,
And if I sleep, count me an idle lover;
Admit I sleep, I'll still pursue the theme,
And eagerly I'll kiss thee in a dream . . .

ANONYMOUS, in *Wit's Recreations*, 1641

Andantino

I will give my love an ap—ple with
My head is the ap—ple with

out e'er a core, I will give my love a house~ with
out e'er a core, My mind is the house~ with

out e'er a door, I will give my love a pal—ace wher
out e'er a door, My heart is the pal—ace wher

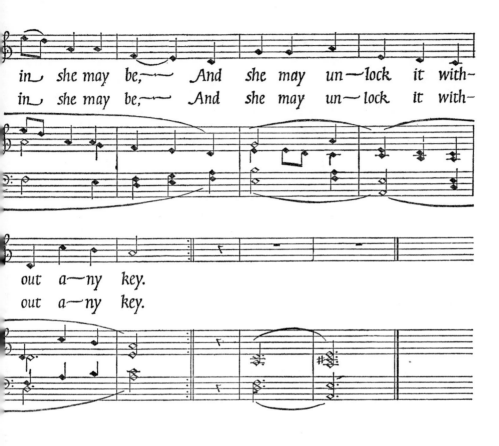

in͜ she may be,‿ And she may un‑lock it with‑
in͜ she may be,‿ And she may un‑lock it with‑

out a‑ny key.
out a‑ny key.

OS AND AIR TRADITIONAL   SETTING BY RALPH VAUGHAN WILLIAMS

A HAPPY MISTRESS

Mrs. Jordan ... though she was neither beautiful, nor handsome, nor even pretty, nor accomplished, nor 'a lady', nor anything conventional, or *comme il faut* whatsoever, yet was so pleasant, so cordial, so natural, so full of spirits, so healthily constituted in mind and body, had such a shapely leg withal, so charming a voice, and such a happy and happy-making expression of countenance, that she appeared something superior to all those requirements of acceptability, and to hold a patent from Nature herself for our delight and good opinion ... The way in which she would take a friend by the cheek and kiss her, or make up a quarrel with a lover, or coax a guardian into good humour, or sing (without accompaniment) the song of 'Since then I'm doomed', or 'In the dead of the night', trusting, as she had a right to do, and as the house wished her to do, to the sole effect of her sweet, mellow and loving voice—the reader will pardon me, but tears of pleasure and regret come into my eyes at the recollection, as if she personified whatsoever was happy at that period of life, and which has gone like herself. The very sound of the little familiar word *bud* from her lips (the abbreviation of husband) as she packed it closer, as it were, in the utterance, and pouted it up with fondness in the man's face, taking him at the same time by the chin, was a whole concentrated world of the power of loving.

LEIGH HUNT, *Autobiography*, 1850

A MERRY MONARCH

I PASS all my hours in a shady old grove,
And I live not the day that I see not my Love.
I survey every walk now my Phyllis is gone,
And sigh when I think we were there all alone.
    Oh, then 'tis! oh, then I think there's no such hell
    Like loving, like loving too well!

But each shade and each conscious bower when I find,
Where I once have been happy and she has been kind,
And I see the print left of her shape in the green,
And imagine the pleasure may yet come again;
    Oh, then 'tis! oh, then I think no joy's above
    The pleasures, the pleasures of love!

While alone to myself I repeat all her charms,
She I love may be locked in another man's arms:
She may laugh at my cares, and so false she may be
To say all the kind things she before said to me.
    Oh, then 'tis! oh, then I think there's no such hell
    Like loving, like loving too well!

But when I consider the truth of her heart,
Such an innocent passion, so kind, without art,
I fear I have wronged her, and hope she may be
So full of true love to be jealous of me.
    Oh, then 'tis! oh, then I think no joy's above
    The pleasures, the pleasures of love!

Attributed to KING CHARLES II
in *Westminster Drollery*, 1671

WHEN BEAUTY AND BEAUTY MEET

WHEN Beauty and Beauty meet
  All naked, fair to fair,
The earth is crying-sweet,
  And scattering-bright the air,
Eddying, dizzying, closing round
  With soft and drunken laughter;
Veiling all that may befall
  After—after—

Where Beauty and Beauty met,
  Earth's still a-tremble there,
And winds are scented yet,
  And memory-soft the air,
Bosoming, folding glints of light,
  And shreds of shadowy laughter;
Not the tears that fill the years
  After—after—

RUPERT BROOKE
1914 and other Poems, 1915

148

ABUNDANT PLEASURES

HENCE with passion, sighs and tears,
Disasters, sorrows, cares and fears!
See, my Love, my Love, appears,
    That thought himself exiled!
Whence might all these loud joys grow,
Whence might mirth and banquets flow,
But that he's come, he's come, I know?
    Fair Fortune, thou hast smiled.

Give to these blind windows eyes,
Daze the stars and mock the skies,
And let us two, us two, devise
    To lavish our best treasures;
Crown our wishes with content,
Meet our souls in sweet consent,
And let this night, this night, be spent
    In all abundant pleasures.

THOMAS HEYWOOD
A Maidenhead Well Lost, 1634

NUPTIAL SONG

Sigh, heart, and break not; rest, lark, and wake not!
  Day I hear coming to draw my Love away.
As mere-waves whisper, and clouds grow crisper,
  Ah! like a rose he will waken up with day!

In moon-light lonely, he is my Love only,
  I share with none when Luna rides in gray.
As dawn-beams quicken, my rivals thicken,
  The light and deed and turmoil of the day.

To watch my sleeper to me is sweeter,
  Than any waking words my Love can say;
In dream he finds me and closer winds me!
  Let him rest by me a little more and stay . . .

Fair Darkness, measure thine hours, as treasure
  Shed each one slowly from thine urn, I pray;
Hoard in and cover each from my lover;
  I cannot lose him yet: dear night, delay!

Each moment dearer, true-love, lie nearer,
  My hair shall blind thee lest thou see the ray.
My locks encumber thine ears in slumber,
  Lest any bird dare give thee note of day.

He rests so calmly; we lie so warmly;
  Hand within hand, as children after play;—
In shafted amber on roof and chamber
  Dawn enters; my Love wakens; here is day.

JOHN LEICESTER WARREN, LORD DE TABLEY
Poems Dramatic and Lyrical, 1893

LOVE IN A GARDEN

AND now what monarch would not gardener be,
My fair Amanda's stately gait to see?
How her feet tempt! how soft and light she treads,
Fearing to wake the flowers from their beds!
Yet from their sweet green pillows everywhere,
They start and gaze about to see my Fair.
Look at yon flower yonder, how it grows
Sensibly! how it opes its leaves and blows,
Puts its best Easter clothes on, neat and gay:
Amanda's presence makes it holiday!
Look how on tiptoe that fair lily stands
To look on thee, and court thy whiter hands
To gather it! I saw in yonder crowd—
That tulip bed of which Dame Flora's proud—
A short dwarf flower did enlarge its stalk,
And shoot an inch to see Amanda walk.
Nay, look, my Fairest! look how fast they grow
Into a scaffold-method spring, as though,
Riding to Parliament, were to be seen
In pomp and state some royal amorous Queen!
The gravelled walks, though even as a die,
Lest some loose pebble should offensive lie,
Quilt themselves o'er with downy moss for thee;
The walls are hanged with blossomed tapestry
To hide their nakedness when looked upon;
The maiden fig tree puts Eve's apron on;
The broad-leaved sycamore, and every tree,
Shakes like the trembling asp, and bends to thee,
And each leaf proudly strives, with fresher air
To fan the curlëd tresses of thy hair.

Nay, and the bee too, with his wealthy thigh,
Mistakes his hive, and to thy lips doth fly,
Willing to treasure up his honey there,
Where honey-combs so sweet and plenty are.
Look how that pretty modest columbine
Hangs down its head, to view those feet of thine!
See the fond motion of the strawberry,
Creeping on th' earth, to go along with thee!
The lovely violet makes after too,
Unwilling yet, my dear, to part with you;
The knot-grass and the daisies catch thy toes,
To kiss my fair one's feet before she goes;
All court and wish me lay Amanda down,
And give my dear a new green-flowered gown.
    Come, let me kiss thee falling, kiss at rise,
    Thou in the garden, I in Paradise.

NATHANIEL HOOKES, *Amanda*, 1653

ENGLISH EMBROIDERED PICTURE, *c.* 1660

LIVERPOOL DELFT DISH, *c.* 1760

CAPTIVE

I DID but look and love awhile,
   'Twas but for one half-hour;
Then to resist I had no will,
   And now I have no power.

THOMAS OTWAY
in *The Works of Rochester and
Roscommon*, 1709

I AM half distracted, captain Shandy, said Mrs.Wadman, holding up her cambrick handkerchief to her left eye, as she approach'd the door of my uncle Toby's sentry-box—a mote—or sand—or something— I know not what, has got into this eye of mine—do look into it—it is not in the white—

In saying which, Mrs. Wadman edged herself close in beside my uncle Toby, and squeezing herself down upon the corner of his bench, she gave him an opportunity of doing it without rising up— Do look into it—said she.

Honest soul! thou didst look into it with as much innocency of heart, as ever child look'd into a raree-shew-box; and 'twere as much a sin to have hurt thee.

If a man will be peeping of his own accord into things of that nature—I've nothing to say to it—

My uncle Toby never did: and I will answer for him, that he would have sat quietly upon a sofa from June to January (which, you know, takes in both the hot and cold months), with an eye as fine as the Thracian Rodope's beside him, without being able to tell, whether it was a black or a blue one.

The difficulty was to get my uncle Toby to look at one at all.

'Tis surmounted. And

I see him yonder with his pipe pendulous in his hand, and the ashes falling out of it—looking—and looking—then rubbing his eyes —and looking again, with twice the good-nature that ever Gallileo look'd for a spot in the sun.

In vain! for by all the powers which animate the organ—Widow Wadman's left eye shines this moment as lucid as her right—there is neither mote, or sand, or dust, or chaff, or speck, or particle of opake matter floating in it—there is nothing, my dear paternal uncle! but one lambent delicious fire, furtively shooting out from every part of it, in all directions, into thine—

If thou lookest, uncle Toby, in search of this mote one moment longer—thou art undone.

An eye is for all the world exactly like a cannon, in this respect; That it is not so much the eye or the cannon, in themselves, as it is the carriage of the eye—and the carriage of the cannon, by which both the one and the other are enabled to do so much execution . . .

I protest, Madam, said my uncle Toby, I see nothing whatever in your eye.

It is not in the white; said Mrs. Wadman: my uncle Toby look'd with might and main into the pupil—

Now of all the eyes which ever were created—from your own, Madam, up to those of Venus herself, which certainly were as venereal a pair of eyes as ever stood in a head—there never was an eye of them all, so fitted to rob my uncle Toby of his repose, as the very eye, at which he was looking—it was not, Madam, a rolling eye—a romping or a wanton one—nor was it an eye sparkling—petulant or imperious—of high claims and terrifying exactions, which would have curdled at one that milk of human nature, of which my uncle Toby was made up—but 'twas an eye full of gentle salutations—and soft responses—speaking—not like the trumpet stop of some ill-made organ, in which many an eye I talk to, holds coarse converse—but whispering soft—like the last low accents of an expiring saint—'How can you live comfortless, captain Shandy, and alone, without a bosom to lean your head on—or trust your cares to?'

It was an eye—

But I shall be in love with it myself, if I say another word about it.

It did my uncle Toby's business.

LAURENCE STERNE, *Tristram Shandy*, Book VIII, 1765

FACE TO FACE

When our two souls stand up erect and strong,
  Face to face, silent, drawing nigh and nigher,
  Until the lengthening wings break into fire
At either curvëd point,—what bitter wrong
Can the earth do us, that we should not long
  Be here contented? Think! In mounting higher,
  The angels would press on us, and aspire
To drop some golden orb of perfect song
Into our deep, dear silence. Let us stay
  Rather on earth, Belovëd—where the unfit
Contrarious moods of men recoil away
  And isolate pure spirits, and permit
A place to stand and love in for a day,
  With darkness and the death-hour rounding it.

ELIZABETH BARRETT BROWNING
Sonnets from the Portuguese, 1830

AND IS IT NIGHT?

AND is it night? Are they thine eyes that shine?
  Are we alone and here? and here alone?
May I come near? May I but touch thy shrine?
  Is jealousy asleep or is he gone?
O gods! no more silence my lips with thine,
Lips, kisses, joys, hap—blessings most divine.

Oh come, my dear, our griefs are turned to night,
  And night to joys: night blinds pale envy's eyes:
Silence and sleep prepare us our delight:
  Oh cease we then our woes, our griefs, our cries:
Oh vanish words! words do but passions move:
O dearest life, joy's sweet, O sweetest love!

ANONYMOUS, set to music by
Robert Jones in *A Musical Dream*, 1609

OCTOBER TUNE

O LOVE, turn from the unchanging sea, and gaze
Down these grey slopes upon the year grown old,
A-dying mid the autumn-scented haze
That hangeth o'er the hollow in the wold,
Where the wind-bitten ancient elms infold
Grey church, long barn, orchard, and red-roofed stead,
Wrought in dead days for men a long while dead.

Come down, O love; may not our hands still meet,
Since still we live today, forgetting June,
Forgetting May, deeming October sweet—
—Oh hearken, hearken! through the afternoon,
The grey tower sings a strange old tinkling tune!
Sweet, sweet, and sad, the toiling year's last breath,
Too satiate of life to strive with death.

And we too—will it not be soft and kind,
That rest from life, from patience and from pain,
That rest from bliss we know not when we find,
That rest from love which ne'er the end can gain?—
—Hark, how the tune swells, that erewhile did wane!
Look up, love!—ah, cling close and never move!
How can I have enough of life and love?

WILLIAM MORRIS
The Earthly Paradise, 1870

THE FAITHFUL AND THE TRUE

LOVE lives beyond
The tomb, the earth, which fades like dew!
I love the fond,
The faithful, and the true.

Love lives in sleep,
The happiness of healthy dreams:
Eve's dews may weep,
But love delightful seems.

'Tis seen in flowers,
And in the morning's pearly dew;
In earth's green hours,
And in the heaven's eternal blue.

'Tis heard in Spring
When light and sunbeams, warm and kind,
On angel's wing
Bring love and music to the mind.

And where is voice,
So young, so beautiful, and sweet
As Nature's choice,
Where Spring and lovers meet?

Love lives beyond
The tomb, the earth, the flowers, and dew
I love the fond,
The faithful, young and true.

JOHN CLARE, *Life and Remains*, 1873

LOVE'S MATRIMONY

THERE is no happy life
But in a wife;
The comforts are so sweet
When they do meet:
'Tis plenty, peace, a calm
Like dropping balm:
Love's weather is so fair,
Perfumèd air,
Each word such pleasure brings
Like soft-touched strings;
Love's passion moves the heart
On either part.
Such harmony together,
So pleased in either,
No discords, concords still,
Sealed with one will.

By love, God man made one,
Yet not alone:
Like stamps of king and queen
It may be seen,
Two figures but one coin;
So they do join,
Only they not embrace,
We, face to face.

WILLIAM CAVENDISH
DUKE OF NEWCASTLE
The Phanseys, c. 1645

LOVE LESSON

AFTER I was married, and had brought my wife home to Cambridge, it so fell out that one rainy morning I stayed within, and in my chamber. My wife and I were all alone, she intent upon her needle-works and I playing upon my lute at the table by her.

She sat very still and quiet, listening to all I played without a word a long time, till at last I happened to play this Lesson, which, so soon as I had once played, she earnestly desired me to play it again. 'For,' said she, 'that shall be called My Lesson'. From which words, so spoken, with emphasis and accent, it presently came into my remembrance the time when and the occasion of its being produced, and returned her this answer, viz. that 'It may very properly be called Your Lesson, for when I composed it you were wholly in my fancy and the chief object and ruler of my thoughts'.

THOMAS MACE, *Musick's Monument*, 1676

VIII: DREAMING

THERE is more pleasure in building castles in the air than on the ground.

EDWARD GIBBON, *Miscellaneous Works*, 1796

MAN is a *make-believe* animal—he is never so truly himself as when he is acting a part.

WILLIAM HAZLITT, *Notes of a Journey through France and Italy*, 1826

I SOMETIMES feel a little uneasy about that imagined self of mine—the Me of my daydreams—who leads a melodramatic life of his own, out of all relation with my real existence. So one day I shadowed him down the street. He loitered along for a while, and then stood at a shop-window and dressed himself out in a gaudy tie and yellow waistcoat. Then he bought a great sponge and two stuffed birds and took them to his lodgings, where he led a shady existence. Next he moved to a big house in Mayfair, and gave grand dinner-parties, with splendid service and costly wines. His amorous adventures among the High-up Ones of this Earth I pass over. He soon sold his house and horses, gave up his motors, dismissed his retinue of servants, and went—saving two young ladies from being run over on the way—to live a life of heroic self-sacrifice among the poor.

I was beginning to feel encouraged about him, when, in passing a fishmonger's, he pointed at a great salmon and said, 'I caught that fish'.

LOGAN PEARSALL SMITH, *Trivia*, 1918

WHEN my cousin and I took our porridge of a morning, we had a device to enliven the course of the meal. He ate his with sugar, and explained it to be a country continually buried under snow. I took mine with milk, and explained it to be a country suffering gradual inundation. You can imagine us exchanging bulletins; how here was an island still unsubmerged, here a valley not yet covered with snow; what inventions were made; how his population lived in cabins on perches and travelled on stilts, and how mine was always in boats; how the interest grew furious, as the last corner of safe ground was cut off on all sides and grew smaller every moment; and how, in fine, the food was of altogether secondary importance, and might even have been nauseous, so long as we seasoned it with these dreams. But perhaps the most exciting moments I ever had over a meal were in the case of calves' foot jelly. It was hardly possible not to believe— and you may be sure, so far from trying, I did all I could to favour the illusion—that some part of it was hollow, and that sooner or later my spoon would lay open the secret tabernacle of the golden rock. There might some miniature Red Beard await his hour; there might one find the treasures of the Forty Thieves, and bewildered Cassim beating about the walls. And so I quarried on slowly, with bated breath, savouring the interest. Believe me, I had little palate left for the jelly; and though I preferred the taste when I took cream with it, I used often to go without, because the cream dimmed the transparent fractures.

ROBERT LOUIS STEVENSON
Virginibus Puerisque, 1881

TRANSFORMATION SCENES

ONE morning when I was in the wood something happened which
was nothing less than a transformation of myself and the world,
although I 'believed' nothing new. I was looking at a great, spreading, bursting oak. The first tinge from the greenish-yellow buds
was just visible. It seemed to be no longer a tree away from me and
apart from me. The enclosing barriers of consciousness were re-
moved and the text came into my mind, 'Thou in me and I in Thee'.
The distinction of self and not-self was an illusion. I could feel the
rising sap; in me also sprang the fountain of life uprushing from its
roots, and the joy of its outbreak at the extremity of each twig right
up to the summit was my own: that which kept me apart was
nothing.

MARK RUTHERFORD
More Pages from a Journal, 1910

WHEN I was but thirteen or so
  I went into a golden land
Chimborazo, Cotopaxi
  Took me by the hand.

My father died, my brother too,
  They passed like fleeting dreams,
I stood where Popocatapetl
  In the sunlight gleams.

I dimly heard the master's voice
  And boys far-off at play,
Chimborazo, Cotopaxi
  Had stolen me away.

166

I walked in a great golden dream
  To and fro from school—
Shining Popocatepatl
  The dusty streets did rule.

I walked home with a gold dark boy
  And never a word I'd say,
Chimborazo, Cotopaxi
  Had taken my speech away:

I gazed entranced upon his face
  Fairer than any flower—
O shining Popocatapetl
  It was thy magic hour:

The houses, people, traffic seemed
  Thin fading dreams by day,
Chimborazo, Cotopaxi
  They had stolen my soul away!

w. j. turner, 'Romance', *The Hunter*, 1916

THE MOOD OF DREAM

ALL day long the door of the sub-conscious remains just ajar; we slip through to the other side, and return again, as easily and secretly as a cat. A dreamlike mood will haunt the mind as moonlight through a window haunts a room, or the sense of disquietude and foreboding that foretells a storm. Obsessive memories vividly imagined, welcome or unwelcome, will insinuate themselves into our active and open thoughts, and so at length decoy our attention to them. As may the distant singing of a bird which the ear, at first refusing to heed, at length cannot evade; as does the shadow-barred light on the wall in Rembrandt's picture—patiently waiting until St. Jerome peers up from his great open book to welcome its company. Any glimpse of unexpected beauty, that of a lovely face, or of a serene landscape, its hollows receding beyond low hills, or of a tranquil daybreak and an eastern sky with its dove-grey low-lying lattice of clouds, the pale blue as of an infinite peace between them— all such things, even an abstracted moment with a pebble, a tea-cup, or a blade of grass, may still the waking mind, and so are reminiscent of the more tranquil and moving of our dreams.

WALTER DE LA MARE, *Behold, this Dreamer!* 1939

THE FLAME IN THE PETALS

... As he walked one evening, a garden gate, usually closed, stood open; and lo! within, a great red hawthorn, in full flower, embossing heavily the bleached and twisted trunk and branches, so aged that there were but few green leaves thereon—a plumage of tender, crimson fire out of the heart of the dry wood. The perfume of the tree had now and again reached him, in the currents of the wind, over the wall, and he had wondered what might be behind it, and was now allowed to fill his arms with the flowers—flowers enough for all the old blue-china pots along the chimney-piece, making fête in the children's room. Was it some periodic moment in the expansion of soul within him, or mere trick of heat in the heavily-laden summer air? But the beauty of the thing struck home to him feverishly, and in dreams, all night, he loitered along a magic roadway of crimson flowers, which seemed to open ruddily in thick, fresh masses about his feet, and fill softly all the little hollows in the banks on either side. Always, afterwards, summer by summer, as the flowers came on, the blossom of the red hawthorn still seemed to him absolutely the reddest of all things; and the goodly crimson, still alive in the works of old Venetian masters, or old Flemish tapestries, called out always from afar the recollection of the flame in those perishing little petals, as it pulsed gradually out of them, kept long in the drawers of an old cabinet.

WALTER PATER, *The Child in the House*, 1894

169

GLIMMERINGS

FLUTTER of something in the past, that made
A light of white across the flickering shade;
   That passed us near, but will come back no more.

Shudder of something in the days that are:
Possible music in sweet notes that jar:
   And not unlike some notes we heard before.

Visible glimpses of old robes again:
Audible echoes of old sounds, with pain
   And distance touched, but playing o'er and o'er.

As if love might have been, and has not been:
As if love yet, though faint, in hope were seen:
   A far, faint flicker, down a lonely shore.

O follow, follow, and find it! o'er the slope
Of matted sands, before the tide come up!
   Ere night close soon, and it be seen no more!

THOMAS ASHE, *Dryope*, 1861

THE FAIRY FELLER'S MASTERSTROKE
PAINTING BY RICHARD DADI
1858–6.

GREENWICH (DETAIL): PAINTING BY J. J. J. TISSOT

DAY-DREAMING

THIS placid pastime—snare of the idle, scorn of the matter-of-fact—deserves a slender anthology all to itself. It has indeed been recently scrutinized, dissected, and tabulated in more than one treatise slender neither in bulk nor argumentation. Compared with dream, it is what nectar is to honey, tint to colour. It resembles, in its gentle rilling, the circulation of the blood; and *may* be the usual occupation, apart from the needs and dangers of their workaday existence, of bird and beast and fish. A passive looking-glass-life of active reflections—the cow in the meadow, the sheep in the corn. A Painted Lady perched on a flower; a thrush in tranced meditation on her nest; a drowsy cat on her footstool by the fire, are, at least, pictures and emblems of reverie; and a great deal more of our workaday life is spent in this heedless industry that we are likely to realize, or might care to confess. The enjoyment of every tale, of every poem we read, indeed, is largely in the nature of a day-dream, even though it is being built up in an astonishing fashion out of a purely verbal fabric. Every hope, every expectation, every desire and resolve concerning that radiant or dismal region of the life of the mind which we call the Future, and which, in general, might be more precisely designated as the Never-Never-Land, also resembles a day-dream—suspended, like dew-drops, on filaments of fact and truth and fancy, spun out of the silk of memory, and even more flimsy, if no less attractive in design, than a spider's web. 'That it was May, thus dremëd', whispers romance, and Cupid creeps a little closer with his dart.

WALTER DE LA MARE, *Behold, this Dreamer!* 1939

THE RULE OF IMAGINATION

MEN are ruled by imagination: imagination makes them into men, capable of madness and of immense labours. We work dreaming. Consider what dreams must have dominated the builders of the Pyramids—dreams geometrical, dreams funereal, dreams of resurrection, dreams of outdoing the pyramid of some other Pharaoh! What dreams occupy that fat man in the street, toddling by under his shabby hat and bedraggled rain-coat? Perhaps he is in love; perhaps he is a Catholic, and imagines that early this morning he has partaken of the body and blood of Christ; perhaps he is a revolutionist, with the millenium in his heart and a bomb in his pocket. The spirit bloweth where it listeth; the wind of inspiration carries our dreams before it and constantly refashions them like clouds. Nothing could be madder, more irresponsible, more dangerous than this guidance of men by dreams. What saves us is the fact that our imaginations, groundless and chimerical as they may seem, are secretly suggested and controlled by shrewd old instincts of our animal nature, and by continual contact with things. The shock of sense, breaking in upon us with a fresh irresistible image, checks wayward imagination and sends it rebounding in a new direction, perhaps more relevant to what is happening in the world outside.

When I speak of being governed by imagination, of course I am indulging in a figure of speech, in an ellipsis; in reality we are governed by that perpetual latent process within us by which imagination itself is created. Actual imaginings—the cloud-like thoughts drifting by—are not masters over themselves nor over anything else. They are like the sound of chimes in the night; they know nothing of whence they came, how they will fall out, or how long they will ring. There is a mechanism in the church tower; there was a theme in the composer's head; there is a beadle who has been winding the thing up. The sound wafted to us, muffled by distance and a thousand obstacles, is but the last lost emanation of this magical bell-ringing. Yet in our dream it is all in all; it is what first entertains and absorbs the mind. Imagination, when it chimes within us, apparently of itself, is no less elaborately grounded; it is a last symptom, a rolling echo, by which we detect and name the obscure operation that occasions it; and not this echo in its aesthetic impotence, but the whole operation whose last witness it is, receives in science the name of imagination, and may be truly said to rule the human world . . .

Whilst dreams entertain us, the balance of our character is shifting beneath: we are growing while we sleep. The young think in one way, the drunken in another, and the dead not at all; and I imagine— for I have imagination myself—that they do not die because they stop thinking, but they stop thinking because they die. How much veering and luffing before they make that port! The brain of man, William James used to say, has a hair-trigger organization. His life is terribly experimental. He is perilously dependent on the oscillations of a living needle, imagination, that never points to the true north . . .

Imagination changes the scale of everything, and makes a thousand patterns of the woof of nature, without disturbing a single thread. Or rather—since it is nature itself that imagines—it turns to music what was only strain; as if the universal vibration, suddenly ashamed of having been so long silent and useless, had burst into tears and laughter at its own folly, and in so doing had become wise.

GEORGE SANTAYANA, *Soliloquies in England*, 1922

THE WRITING OF *KUBLA KHAN*

IN the summer of the year 1797, the Author, then in ill health, had retired to a lonely farm-house between Porlock and Linton, on the Exmoor confines of Somerset and Devonshire. In consequence of a slight indisposition an anodyne had been prescribed, from the effects of which he fell asleep in his chair at the moment that he was reading the following sentence, or words of the same substance, in Purchas's Pilgrimage: 'Here the Khan Kubla commanded a palace to be built, and a stately garden thereunto. And thus ten miles of fertile ground were enclosed with a wall.' The author continued for about three hours in a profound sleep, at least of the external senses, during which time he has the most vivid confidence that he could not have composed less than from two to three hundred lines; if that indeed can be called composition in which all the images rose up before him as things, with a parallel production of the correspondent expressions, without any sensation or consciousness of effort. On awaking he appeared to himself to have a distinct recollection of the whole, and taking his pen, ink, and paper, instantly and eagerly wrote down the lines that are here preserved. At this moment he was unfortunately called out by a person on business from Porlock, and detained by him above an hour, and on his return to his room, found, to his no small surprise and mortification, that though he still retained some vague and dim recollection of the general purport of the vision, yet, with the exception of some eight or ten scattered lines and images, all the rest had passed away like the images on the surface of a stream into which a stone has been cast, but, alas! without the after-restoration of the latter!

SAMUEL TAYLOR COLERIDGE
Prefatory note to *Kubla Khan*, 1816
(written in 1798)

FLIGHT OF FANCY

NOTHING is more common, or usually more pleasant, than to dream of flying. It is one of the best specimens of the race; for besides being agreeable, it is made up of the dreams of ordinary life and those of surprising combination. Thus the dreamer sometimes thinks he is flying in unknown regions, sometimes skimming only a few inches above the ground, and wondering he never did it before. He will even dream that he is dreaming about it; and yet is so fully convinced of its feasibility, and so astonished at his never having hit upon so delightful a truism, that he is resolved to practise it the moment he wakes. 'One has only', says he, 'to give a little spring with one's foot, so, and—oh! it's the easiest and most obvious thing in the world. I'll always skim hereafter'. We dreamt once that a woman set up some Flying Rooms, as a person does a tavern. We went to try them, and nothing could be more satisfactory and commonplace on all sides. The landlady welcomed us with a courtesy, hoped for friends and favours, etc., and then showed us into a spacious room, not round, as might be expected, but long, and after the usual dining fashion. 'Perhaps, sir', said she, 'you would like to try the room.' Upon which we made no more ado, but sprung up and made two or three genteel circuits, now taking the height of it, like a house-lark, and then cutting the angles, like a swallow. 'Very pretty flying indeed' said we, 'and very moderate.'

LEIGH HUNT, 'Of Dreams'
in *The Indicator*, Oct. 18, 1820

IX : MAKING

LOUIS DUBEDAT: I believe in Michael Angelo, Velasquez, and Rembrandt; in the might of design, the mystery of colour, the redemption of all things by Beauty everlasting, and the message of Art that has made these hands blessed. Amen.

BERNARD SHAW, *The Doctor's Dilemma*, 1906

IF a man love the labour of any trade, apart from any question of success or fame, the gods have called him.

ROBERT LOUIS STEVENSON

THE sound of tools to a clever workman who loves his work is like the tentative sounds of the orchestra to the violinist who has to bear his part in the overture; the strong fibres begin their accustomed thrill, and what was a moment before joy, vexation or ambition, begins its change into energy. All passion becomes strength when it has an outlet from the narrow limits of our personal lot in the labour of our right arm, the cunning of our right hand, or the still, creative activity of our thought.

GEORGE ELIOT, *Adam Bede*, 1859

A TOOL is but the extension of a man's hand, and a machine is but a complex tool, and he that invents a machine augments the power of a man.

HENRY WARD BEECHER, *Eyes and Ears*, 1862

... AND in the heat of the furnace will he wrestle with his work: the noise of the hammer will be in his ear, and his eyes upon the pattern of the vessel; he will set his heart upon perfecting his works ...

Ecclesiasticus

THINGS men have made with wakened hands, and put soft life into are awake through years with transferred touch, and go on glowing for long years.
And for this reason, some old things are lovely,
warm still with the life of forgotten men who made them.

D. H. LAWRENCE, *Pansies*, 1929

THE first blow of the domed hammer into the virgin whiteness of the metal; the rhythmic beating of steel hammer to steel anvil—making the metal obey his will and bringing the inert, flat, circular piece of metal up to a faultless body of a drinking cup, a chalice, or a large fruit or flower bowl; the choice of strengthening wires made on a draw bench as it was three hundred years ago; the extreme care and patience necessary to fit the base to the body; the feeling of fire responding to his will when fusing the two parts together; its cleanliness of working, for there is no dross when handling silver; the exhilaration of decorating by engraving or chasing; and finally the feel of the finished piece—all these are the simple joys of the craftsman.

LESLIE DURBIN
in *Fifteen Craftsmen on their Crafts*, 1948

179

GATHERED RAYS

WE will entangle buds and flowers and beams
Which twinkle on the fountain's brim, and make
Strange combinations out of common things,
Like human babes in their brief innocence;
And we will search, with looks and words of love,
For hidden thoughts, each lovelier than the last,
Our unexhausted spirits; and like lutes,
Touched by the skill of the enamoured wind,
Weave harmonies divine, yet ever new,
From difference sweet where discord cannot be;
And hither come, sped on the charmëd winds,
Which meet from all the points of heaven, as bees
From every flower aereal Enna feeds,
At their known island-homes in Himera,
The echoes of the human world, which tell
Of the low voice of love, almost unheard,
And dove-eyed pity's murmured pain, and music,
Itself the echo of the heart, and all
That tempers or improves man's life, now free;
And lovely apparitions,—dim at first,
Then radiant, as the mind, arising bright
From the embrace of beauty (whence the forms
Of which these are the phantoms) casts on them
The gathered rays which are reality—
Shall visit us, the progeny immortal
Of Painting, Sculpture, and rapt Poesy,
And arts, though unimagined, yet to be.

PERCY BYSSHE SHELLEY
Prometheus Unbound, 1820

MUSIC IN THE MIND

I CARRY my ideas about me for a long time, often a very long time, before I commit them to writing. My memory is so good that I never forget a theme that has once come to me, even if it is a matter of years. I alter much, reject, try again until I am satisfied. Then, in my head, the thing develops in all directions, and, since I know precisely what I want, the original idea never eludes me. It rises before me, grows, I hear it, see it in all its size and extension, standing before me like a cast, and it only remains for me to write it down, which is soon done when I can find the time, for sometimes I take up other work, though I never confuse that with the other. You will ask where I find my ideas: I hardly know. They come uninvited, directly or indirectly. I can almost grasp them with my hands in the open air, in the woods, while walking, in the stillness of the night, early in the morning, called up by moods which the poet translates into words, I into musical tones. They ring and roar and swirl about me until I write them down in notes.

LUDWIG VAN BEETHOVEN
Recorded in Alexander Wheelock Thayer's *Life*, 1866

HE is the only person I ever knew who answered to the idea of a man of genius . . . His voice rolled on the ear like the pealing organ, and its sound alone was the music of thought. His mind was clothed with wings; and, raised on them, he lifted philosophy to heaven. In his descriptions, you then saw the progress of human happiness and liberty in bright and never-ending succession, like the steps of Jacob's ladder, with airy shapes ascending and descending, and with the voice of God at the top of the ladder . . .

WILLIAM HAZLITT, on Coleridge
Lectures on the English Poets, 1818

THE POET

FOR me there is no dismay
Though ills enough impend.
I have learned to count each day
Minute by breathing minute—
Birds that lightly begin it,
Shadows muting its end—
As lovers count for luck
Their own heart-beats and believe
In the forest of time they pluck
Eternity's single leaf.

Tonight the moon's at the full.
Full moon's the time for murder.
But I look to the clouds that hide her—
The bay below me is dull,
An unreflecting glass—
And chafe for the clouds to pass,
And wish she suddenly might
Blaze down at me so I shiver
Into a twelve-branched river
Of visionary light.

For now imagination,
My royal, impulsive swan,
With raking flight—I can see her—
Comes down as it were upon
A lake in whirled snow-floss
And flurry of spray like a skier
Checking. Again I feel
The wounded waters heal.
Never before did she cross
My heart with exaltation.

Oh, on this striding edge,
This hare-bell height of calm
Where intuitions swarm
Like nesting gulls and knowledge
Is free as the winds that blow,
A little while sustain me,
Love, till my answer is heard!
Oblivion roars below,
Death's cordon narrows: but vainly,
If I've slipped the carrier word.

Dying, any man may
Feel wisdom harmonious, fateful
At the tip of his dry tongue.
All I have felt or sung
Seems now but the moon's fitful
Sleep on a clouded bay,
Swan's maiden flight, or the climb
To a tremulous, hare-bell crest.
Love, tear the song from my breast!
Short, short is the time.

CECIL DAY-LEWIS
Poems in Wartime, 1940

BEGINNINGS

I WAS for some time kept at reading, writing, and figures—how long, I know not, but I know that as soon as my question was done upon my slate, I spent as much time as I could in filling with my pencil all the unoccupied spaces, with representations of such objects as struck my fancy; and these were rubbed out, for fear of a beating, before my question was given in. As soon as I reached Fractions, Decimals, &c., I was put to learn Latin . . . I rather flagged in this department of my education, and the margins of my books, and every space of spare and blank paper, became filled with various kinds of devices or scenes I had met with; and these were accompanied with wretched rhymes explanatory of them. As soon as I filled all the blank spaces in my books, I had recourse, at all spare times, to the gravestones and the floor of the church porch, with a bit of chalk, to give vent to this propensity of mind of figuring whatever I had seen. At that time I had never heard of the word 'drawing'; nor did I know of any other paintings besides the King's arms in the church, and the signs in Ovingham of the Black Bull, the White Horse, the Salmon, and the Hounds and Hare. I always thought I could make a far better hunting scene that the latter: the others were beyond my hand. I remember once of my master overlooking me while I was very busy with my chalk in the porch, and of his putting me very greatly to the blush by ridiculing me and calling me a conjurer. My father, also, found a deal of fault for 'mispending my time in such idle pursuits'; but my propensity for drawing was so rooted that nothing could deter me from persevering in it; and many of my evenings at home were spent in filling the flags of the floor and the hearth-stone with my chalky designs.

THOMAS BEWICK
A Memoir . . . written by Himself, 1862
(written in 1822)

184

ACHIEVEMENTS

IT was on the day, or rather night, of the 27th of June, 1787, between the hours of eleven and twelve, that I wrote the last lines of the last page, in a summer house in my garden. After laying down my pen I took several turns in a *berceau*, or covered walk of acacias, which commands a prospect of the country, the lake and mountains. The air was temperate, the sky was serene, the silver orb of the moon was reflected from the waters, and all nature was silent. I will not dissemble the first emotions of joy on recovery of my freedom, and perhaps, the establishment of my fame. But my pride was soon humbled, and a sober melancholy was spread over my mind, by the idea that I had taken an everlasting leave of an old and agreeable companion, and that, whatsoever might be the future date of my History, the life of the historian must be short and precarious.

EDWARD GIBBON, *Memoirs*, 1796

THE discovery of the two optically active tartaric acids was a momentous one, effecting a revolution in the views of chemists regarding molecular structure; and we can well understand the feeling of happiness and the nervous excitement by which Pasteur was overcome on making his discovery. Rushing from his laboratory and meeting a curator he embraced him, exclaiming, 'I have just made a great discovery! I have separated the sodium ammonium parotartrate into two salts of opposite action on the plane of polarization of light. The dextro-salt is in all respects identical with the dextro-tartrate. I am so happy and overcome by such nervous excitement that I am unable to place my eye again to the polarization apparatus.'

ALEXANDER FINDLAY, *Chemistry in the Service of Man*, 1916

STONEMASONS

WE have graven the mountain of God with hands,
As our hands were graven of God, they say,
Where the seraphs burn in the sun like brands
And the devils carry the rains away:
Making a thrift of the throats of hell,
Our gargoyles gather the roaring rain,
Whose yawn is more than a frozen yell
And their very vomiting not in vain . . .

We have graven the forest of heaven with hands,
Being great with a mirth too gross for pride,
In the stone that battered him Stephen stands
And Peter himself is petrified:
Such hands as have grubbed in the glebe for bread
Have bidden the blank rock blossom and thrive,
Such hands as have stricken a live man dead
Have struck, and stricken the dead alive . . .

Fold your hands before heaven in praying,
Lift up your hands into heaven and cry;
But look where our dizziest spires are saying
What the hands of a man did up in the sky:
Drenched before you have heard the thunder,
White before you have felt the snow;
For the giants lift up their heads to wonder
How high the hands of a man could go.

G. K. CHESTERTON
The Ballad of St Barbara and Other Verses, 1922

COUNTRY SKILLS

OVER all the countryside, wherever one goes, indications of techniques are visible to the seeing eye. By technique is meant an exercise of skill acquired by practice and directed to a well foreseen end. It is the name for the action of any of our powers after they have been so improved by training as to perform that action with certainty and success. This is the nature of technique; and, go where one will about the country, one can hardly escape the evidences of its abundant practice.

The metalled roads tell of it well. The deep-rutted by-roads, too, and the winding lanes, preserve through years of neglect the traces of technique in their hedgerows, however tangled; in their ditches, however choked. On the old ruinous field gate, with its lightly-arched, tapering top bar rudely carved on the under side against the tenon, the grey lichen cannot hide the signs of a vitality more marvellous than its own—the intensified vitality of those skilled hands that shaped the timbers. The fields, newly ploughed in straight furrows, or with stubble in long rows, or green lines of wheat just appearing after snow; and the meadows, well rolled and level, or perhaps still wavy from long-forgotten ploughings; and the river banks; and the copses growing up on old 'stamms'; and the woods, thinned out, and full of decayed stumps of felled trees, are all witnesses to the exercise of technical powers, just as are the tools, the farm implements, the waggons and carts, the very horses, and cattle, and sheep. Each detail of country life offers its convincing proof of skill to anyone who cares to look.

GEORGE BOURNE, *Lucy Bettesworth*, 1913

THE FARMER

BUT turn, my Muse, nor let th'alluring form
Of beauty lead too far thy devious steps.
See where the farmer, with a master's eye,
Surveys his little kingdom, and exults
In sov'reign independence. At a word,
His feathery subjects in obedience flock
Around his feeding hand, who in return
Yield a delicious tribute to his board,
And o'er his couch their downy plumage spread.
The peacock here expands his eyeful plumes,
A glittering pageant, to the mid-day sun:
In the stiff awkwardness of foolish pride,
The swelling turkey apes his stately step,
And calls the bristling feathers round his head.
There the loud herald of the morning struts
Before his cackling dames, the passive slaves
Of his promiscuous pleasure. O'er the pond,
See the grey gander, with his female train,
Bending their lofty necks; and gabbling ducks,
Rejoicing on the surface clap their wings;
Whilst wheeling round, in airy wanton flights,
The glossy pigeons chase their sportive loves,
Or in soft cooings tell their amorous tale.
Here stacks of hay, there pyramids of corn,
Promise the future market large supplies:
While with an eye of triumph he surveys
His piles of wood, and laughs at winter's frown . . .

ROBERT DODSLEY, *Public Virtue*, 1753

HARVESTING IN BRITTANY
PAINTING BY PAUL GAUGUIN, 188

THE LACE-MAKER: PAINTING BY CASPAR NETSCHER 1664

THE ARTIST'S INSIGHT

WE carve and paint, or we behold what is carved and painted, as students of the mystery of Form. The virtue of art lies in detachment, in sequestering one object from the embarrassing variety. Until one thing comes out from the connection of things, there can be enjoyment, contemplation, but no thought. Our happiness and unhappiness are unproductive. The infant lies in a pleasing trance, but his individual character and his practical power depend on his daily progress in the separation of things, and dealing with one at a time. Love and all the passions concentrate all existence around a single form. It is the habit of certain minds to give an all-excluding fullness to the object, the thought, the word, they alight upon, and to make that for the time the deputy of the world. These are the artists, the orators, the leaders of society. The power to detach, and to magnify by detaching, is the essence of rhetoric in the hands of the orator and the poet. This rhetoric, or power to fix the momentary eminency of an object,—so remarkable in Burke, in Byron, in Carlyle,—the painter and sculptor exhibit in colour and in stone. The power depends on the depth of the artist's insight of that object he contemplates. For every object has its roots in central nature, and may of course be so exhibited to us as to represent the world.

RALPH WALDO EMERSON, from 'Art', *Essays*, 1841

WHEN out of the riot of forms and colours in nature the artificer is able to co-ordinate the elements of a more comprehensible design, then it is that for brief moments he reaches harmony with the universal spirit. Sometimes in those seconds of insight time stands still, events past, present and future remain stationary like resting cattle spotted on the surface of a field, and the artist sees them as God sees time.

ROBERT GIBBINGS, in *Sermons by Artists*, 1934

THE GARDENER

THE most exquisite delights of sense are pursued in the contrivance and planning of gardens, which, with fruits, flowers, shades, fountains, and the music of birds that frequent such happy places, seem to furnish all the pleasures of the several senses, and with the greatest, or at least the most natural perfections.

SIR WILLIAM TEMPLE, *Miscellanea*, 1690

Is it not a pleasant sight to behold a multitude of trees round about, in decent form and order, bespangled and gorgeously apparelled with green leaves, blooms and goodly fruits as with a rich robe of embroidered work, or as hanging with some precious and costly jewels or pearls, the boughs laden and burdened, bowing down to you, and freely offering their ripe fruits as a large satisfaction of all your labours?

RALPH AUSTEN, *A Treatise of Fruit-Trees*, 1653

ALL the wars of the world, all the Caesars, have not the staying power of a lily in a cottage border . . . The immortality of marbles and of miseries is a vain, small thing compared to the immortality of a flower that blooms and is dead by dusk.

REGINALD FARRER, *The Rainbow Bridge*, 1921

THAT border was a dream in June. It is going to be lovely again in October.

RUTH DRAPER

I took money and bought flowering trees
And planted them out on the bank to the east of the Keep.
I simply bought whatever had most blooms,
Not caring whether peach, apricot, or plum.
A hundred fruits, all mixed up together;
A thousand branches, flowering in due rotation.
Each has its season coming early or late;
But to all alike the fertile soil is kind.
The red flowers hang like a heavy mist;
The white flowers gleam like a fall of snow.
The wandering bees cannot bear to leave them;
The sweet birds also come there to roost.
In front there flows an ever-running stream;
Beneath there is built a little flat terrace.
Sometimes I sweep the flagstones of the terrace;
Sometimes, in the wind, I raise my cup and drink.
The flower-branches screen my head from the sun;
The flower-buds fall down into my lap.
Alone drinking, alone singing my songs,
I do not notice that the moon is level with the steps.
The people of Pa do not care for flowers;
All the spring no one has come to look.
But their Governor-General, alone with his cup of wine,
Sits till evening, and will not move from the place!

Written when Governor of Chung-Chou in the mid-ninth
century AD by PO-CHÜ-I, translated by ARTHUR WALEY
170 Chinese Poems, 1920

X : UNDERSTANDING

WHEN the soul attends through her proper faculty, she is instantly carried away into the other world of purity, eternity, immortality and of unchanging things; and there finding her own element she merges herself in it (that is, so long as she is true to herself and keeps herself whole); and she strays no longer, but thus always in regard to it she remains steadfast, for that also in which she has merged herself is steadfast. And the name of this condition of the Soul is Understanding.

PLATO, *Phaedo*
Translated by Robert Bridges

I AM sure there is a common spirit that plays within us, yet makes no part of us; and that is, the Spirit of God, the fire and scintillation of that noble and mighty Essence, which is the life and radical heat of Spirits, and those essences that know not the vertue of the Sun; a fire quite contrary to the fire of Hell. This is that gentle heat that brooded on the waters, and in six days hatched the World; this is that irradiation that dispels the mists of Hell, the clouds of horror, fear, sorrow, despair, and preserves the region of the mind in serenity. Whosoever feels not the warm gale and gentle ventilation of this Spirit, though I feel his pulse, I dare not say he lives: for truly, without this, there is no heat under the Tropick; nor any light, though I dwelt in the body of the Sun.

SIR THOMAS BROWNE, *Religio Medici*, 1642

THE whole natural world corresponds to the spiritual world, not only in general but also in particular. Whatever, therefore, in the natural world derives its existence from the spiritual, is said to be its correspondent ... The reason for correspondences is that the natural world with all that it contains exists and subsists from the spiritual world, and both worlds from the divine Being. We say subsists as well as exists because every thing subsists from that which gave it existence, subsistence being perpetual existence; and because nothing can subsist from itself but only from something prior to itself, and thus originally from the First Cause; if it were separated from this, it would utterly perish or disappear ...

When the union of good and truth is effected in a man . . . he enters into a state of delight from heavenly peace. This peace may be compared to morning or dawn in spring, when, the night being past, at the rising of the sun everything on earth begins to live anew, the dew which falls from heaven causes plants to diffuse their scent, while the mild vernal temperature imparts fertility to the soil and gladdens the heart of man; and this takes place because morning or dawn, in the time of spring, corresponds to the state of peace of the angels in Heaven.

EMANUEL SWEDENBORG
Heaven, and its Wonders, and Hell, 1758
Translated by Frank Bayley

GOD, in the whizzing of a pleasant wind,
Shall march upon the tops of mulberry trees.

GEORGE PEELE, *David and Bethsabe,* 1599

THE CROWN OF MEEKNESS

THERE is a spirit, which I feel, that delights to do no evil nor to revenge any wrong, but delights to endure all things, in hope to enjoy its own in the end. Its hope is to outlive all wrath and contention, and to weary out all exaltation and cruelty, or whatever is of a nature contrary to itself. It sees to the end of all temptations. As it bears no evil in itself, so it conceives none in thoughts to any other. If it be betrayed, it bears it; for its ground and spring is the mercies and forgiveness of God. Its crown is meekness, its life is everlasting love unfeigned. It takes its kingdom with intreaty and not with contention, and keeps it by lowliness of mind. In God alone it can rejoice, though none else regard it or can own its life. It is conceived in sorrow, and brought forth without any to pity it; nor doth it murmur at grief and oppression. It never rejoiceth but through sufferings: for with the world's joy it is murdered. I found it alone, being forsaken. I have fellowship therein with them who lived in dens and desolate places in the earth, who through death obtained this resurrection and eternal holy life.

JAMES NAYLER, *His Last Testimony,*
said to be delivered by him about two hours before his departure, 1660

O WORLD INVISIBLE

O WORLD invisible, we view thee,
O world intangible, we touch thee,
O world unknowable, we know thee,
Inapprehensible, we clutch thee!

Does the fish soar to find the ocean,
The eagle plunge to find the air—
That we ask of the stars in motion
If they have rumour of thee there?

Not where the wheeling systems darken
And our benumbed conceiving soars!
The drift of pinions, would we hearken,
Beats at our own clay-shuttered doors.

The angels keep their ancient places;—
Turn but a stone, and start a wing!
'Tis ye, 'tis your estrangëd faces,
That miss the many-splendoured thing.

But (when so sad thou canst not sadder)
Cry;—and upon thy so sore loss
Shall shine the traffic of Jacob's ladder
Pitched between Heaven and Charing Cross.

Yea, in the night, my Soul, my daughter,
Cry,—clinging Heaven by the hems;
And lo, Christ walking on the water
Not of Gennesareth, but Thames!

FRANCIS THOMPSON, 'The Kingdom of God'
Works, 1913

SAILING HOMEWARD

CLIFFS that rise a thousand feet
Without a break,
Lake that stretches a hundred miles
Without a wave,
Sands that are white through all the year,
Without a stain,
Pine-tree woods, winter and summer
Ever-green,
Streams that for ever flow and flow
Without a pause,
Trees that for twenty thousand years
Your vows have kept,
You have suddenly healed the pain of a traveller's heart,
And moved his brush to write a new song.

CHAN FANG-SHENG
(fourth century A.D.)
Translated by Arthur Waley
170 Chinese Poems, 1920

PEACE

I SOUGHT for Peace, but could not find;
   I sought it in the city,
But they were of another mind,
   The more's the pity!

I sought for Peace of country swain,
   But yet I could not find;
So I, returning home again,
   Left Peace behind.

Sweet Peace, where dost thou dwell? said I.
   Methought a voice was given;
Peace dwelt not here, long since did fly
   To God in Heaven.

Thought I, this echo is but vain,
   To folly 'tis of kin;
Anon I heard it tell me plain,
   'Twas killed by sin.

Then I believed the former voice,
   And rested well content,
Laid down and slept, rose, did rejoice,
   And then to heaven went.

There I enquired for Peace, and found it true,
An heavenly plant it was, and sweetly grew.

SAMUEL SPEED, *Prison Piety*, 1677

INEBRIATE

I TASTE a liquor never brewed,
From tankards scooped in pearl;
Not all the vats upon the Rhine
Yield such an alcohol!

Inebriate of air am I,
And debauchee of dew,
Reeling, through endless summer days,
From inns of molten blue.

When landlords turn the drunken bee
Out of the foxglove's door,
When butterflies renounce their drams,
I shall but drink the more!

Till seraphs swing their snowy hats,
And saints to windows run,
To see the little tippler
Leaning against the sun!

EMILY DICKINSON
Poems, 1890
(written *c.* 1860)

GOD'S GRANDEUR

THE world is charged with the grandeur of God,
   It will flame out, like shining from shook foil;
   It gathers to a greatness, like the ooze of oil
Crushed. Why do men then now not reck his rod?
Generations have trod, have trod, have trod;
   And all is seared with trade; bleared, smeared with toil;
   And wears man's smudge and shares man's smell: the soil
Is bare now, nor can foot feel, being shod.

And for all this, nature is never spent;
   There lives the dearest freshness deep down things;
And though the last lights off the black West went
   Oh, morning, at the brown brink eastward, springs—
Because the Holy Ghost over the bent
   World broods with warm breast and with ah! bright wings.

GERARD MANLEY HOPKINS
Poems, 1930 (written 1877)

THE SOUL'S BLINDNESS

How is't, my Soul, that thou giv'st eyes their sight
 To view their objects, yet hast none
 To see thine own?
Earth's, air's, heaven's beauties they discern: their light
 Fair flowers admires, their several dresses,
 Their golden tresses;
The lily, rose, the various tulip, scorning
The pride of princes in their choice adorning.

They joy to view the aïr's painted nations:
 The peacock's train, which th'head outvies
 With fairer eyes,
And emulates the heavenly constellations:
 The ostrich, whose fair plume embraves
 Kings, captains, slaves:
The halcyons, whose triton-bills appease
Curled waves, and with their eggs lay stormy seas.

Pilots' fixed eyes observe the arctic Bear,
 With all her unwashed starry trains
 In heavenly plains.
Night-travellers behold the moon to steer
 Her ship, sailing (while Eol raves)
 Through cloudy waves:
Our less world's suns with pleasure view the light
Which gives all beauties beauty, them their sight.

Thou that giv'st sight to clay, to blackness light,
How art so dull, so dim in duty
To view his beauty
Who quickens every life, lights every light?
His height those eagles' eyes surpasses:
Thou wants thy glasses:
Take up that pèrspective and view those streams
Of light, and fill thy waning orb with beams.

Then see the flowers clad in his liveries,
And from his cheek and lovely face
Steal all their grace:
See fowls from him borrow their braveries,
And all their feather-painted dresses
From his fair tresses:
See stars, and moon, the sun and all perfection
Beg light and life from his bright eyes' reflection.

Look on his lips: heaven's gate there open lies,
Thence that grace-breathing Spirit blows,
Thence honey flows.
Look on his hands: the world's full treasuries.
Fix all thy looks his heart upon:
Love's highest throne.
And, when thy sight that radiant beauty blears
And dazzles thy weak eyes, see with thine ears.

PHINEAS FLETCHER
A Father's Testament, 1670
(written before 1640)

THE SPHERE OF THE SPIRIT

Now for my life, it is miracle of thirty years, which to relate were not a history, but a piece of poetry, and would sound to common ears like a fable; for the world, I count it not an Inn, but an Hospital; and a place not to live, but to die in. The world that I regard is my self; it is the microcosm of my own frame that I cast mine eye on: for the other, I use it but like my Globe, and turn it round sometimes for my recreation. Men that look upon my outside, perusing only my condition and fortunes, do err in my Altitude, for I am above Atlas his shoulders. The earth is a point, not only in respect of the Heavens above us, but of that Heavenly and Celestial part within us: that mass of flesh that circumscribes me, limits not my mind; that surface that tells the Heavens it hath an end, cannot persuade me I have any; I take my circle to be above three hundred and sixty; though the number of the arc do measure my body, it comprehendeth not my mind; whilst I study to find how I am a Microcosm, or little world, I find myself something more than the great. There is surely a piece of Divinity in us; something that was before the elements, and owes no homage unto the Sun. Nature tells me I am the Image of God, as well as Scripture: he that understands not thus much hath not his introduction or first lesson, and is yet to begin the Alphabet of man. I am the happiest man alive: I have that in me that can convert poverty into riches, adversity into prosperity: I am more invulnerable than Achilles; Fortune hath not one place to hit me . . . In brief, I am content, and what should Providence add more? Surely this is it we call Happiness, and this do I enjoy: with this I am happy in a dream, and as content to enjoy a happiness in a fancy as others in a more apparent truth and realty.

SIR THOMAS BROWNE, *Religio Medici*, 1642

'...ALL GONE...'

'Age takes in pitiless hands
All one loves most away;
Peace, joy, simplicity
Where then their inward stay?'

Or so, at least they say.

'Marvel of noontide light,
Of gradual break of day;
Dreams, visions of the night
Age withers all away.'

Yes, that is what they say.

'Wonder of winter snow,
Magic of wandering moon,
The starry hosts of heaven—
Come seventy, all are gone.

'Unhappy when alone,
Nowhere at peace to be;
Drowned the old self-sown eager thoughts
Constantly stirring in thee!' . . .

Extraordinary!
That's what they *say* to me!

WALTER DE LA MARE
O Lovely England, 1953

THOUGHTS IN A ROSE GARDEN

THERE is no rose of such vertu
As is the rose that bare Jesu.
    Alleluia.

For in this rose containëd was
Heaven and earth in little space:
    Res miranda.

By that rose we may well see
There be one God in persons three:
    Pares forma.

The angels sungen, the shepherds too:
Gloria in excelsis Deo:
    Gaudeamus.

Leave we all this worldly mirth,
And follow we this joyful birth:
    Transeamus.

ANONYMOUS
(fifteenth century)

THE VIRGI
IN THE ROSE GARDEN
PAINTING BY STEFAN
DA VERON

AN OLD MAN: PAINTING BY REMBRANDT VAN RIJN, *c.* 1632

AFTER THE STORM

THE seas are quiet when the winds give o'er;
So calm are we when passions are no more:
For then we know how vain it was to boast
Of fleeting things, so certain to be lost:
Clouds of affection from our younger eyes
Conceal that emptiness which age descries.

The soul's dark cottage, battered and decayed,
Lets in new light through chinks that time has made
Stronger by weakness: wiser men become,
As they draw near to their eternal home:
Leaving the Old, both Worlds at once they view,
That stand upon the threshold of the New.

EDMUND WALLER, *Poems*, 1686

XI: FALLING ASLEEP

SLEEPY, my dear? Yes, yes, I see
Morpheus is fall'n in love with thee;
Morpheus, my worst of rivals, tries
To draw the curtains of thine eyes,
And fans them with his wing asleep,
Makes drowsy love play at bo-peep;
How prettily his feathers blow
Those fleshy shuttings to and fro!
Oh how he makes me tantalize
With those fair apples of thine eyes,
Equivocates and cheats me still,
Opening and shutting at his will;
Now both, now one, the doting god
Plays with thine eyes at even-and-odd:
My stammering tongue doubts which it might
Bid thee—Good morrow, or Good night;
So thy eyes twinkle, brighter far
Than the bright, trembling evening star;
So a wax taper, burnt within
The socket, plays at out and in.

NATHANIEL HOOKES, *Amanda*, 1653

ONE by one the flowers close,
Lily and dewy rose
Shutting their tender petals from the moon:
The grasshoppers are still; but not so soon
   Are still the noisy crows.

The dormouse squats and eats
Choice little dainty bits
Beneath the spreading roots of a broad lime;
Nibbling his fill he stops from time to time
   And listens where he sits.

From far the lowings come
Of cattle driven home:
From farther still the wind brings fitfully
The vast continual murmur of the sea,
   Now loud, now almost dumb . . .

Hark! that's the nightingale,
Telling the selfsame tale
Her song told when this ancient earth was young;
So echoes answered when her song was sung
   In the first wooded vale.

We call it love and pain
The passion of her strain;
And yet we little understand or know:
Why should it not be rather joy that so
   Throbs in each throbbing vein?

CHRISTINA ROSSETTI, from 'Twilight Calm'
Goblin Market and other Poems, 1862

SETTING BY PETER WARLOCK

thence There may steal an in-fluence All— my powers of care be-

—reav—ing.

II

Though but a shadow, but a sliding,
  Let me know some little joy!
  We, that suffer long annoy,
  Are contented with a thought
  Through an idle fancy wrought:
O let my joys have some abiding!

WORDS BY FRANCIS BEAUMONT, *The Woman-Hater*, 1607

BED

FOR do but consider what an excellent thing sleep is. It is so inestimable a jewel that if a Tyrant would give his crown for an hour's slumber it cannot be bought. Of so beautiful a shape is it that though a man lie with an Empress his heart cannot be at quiet till he leaves her embracements to be at rest with the other. Yea, so greatly indebted are we to this kinsman of death that we owe the better tributary, half of our life, to him: and there is good cause why we should do so, for sleep is that golden chain that ties health and our bodies together. Who complains of want, of wounds, of cares, of great men's oppressions, of captivity, whilst he sleepeth? Beggars in their beds take as much pleasure as kings. Can we therefore surfeit on this delicate ambrosia?

THOMAS DEKKER, *The Gul's Horn-booke*, 1609

My bed, the rest of all my cares,
  The end of toiling pain,
Which bringest ease and solace sweet,
  While darkness doth remain;
My bed, yield to me slumber sweet,
  And trifling dreams repel;
Cause carking care from sobbing breast
  To part, where it doth dwell;
All mockeries of this wretched world
  Put clean from out my mind:
Do these, my bed, and then by thee
  Much comfort shall I find.

TIMOTHY KENDALL
Flowers of Epigrams, 1577

BE STILL, MY SOUL

BE still, my soul. Consider
   The flowers and the stars.
Among these sleeping fragrances,
   Sleep now your cares.
That which the universe
   Lacks room to enclose
Lives in the folded petals
   Of this dark rose.

GERALD BULLETT
'In the Garden at Night'
New Poems, 1949

NOTES ON THE ILLUSTRATIONS

The names of the owners of works illustrated are printed in italics

Half-title page. CARLO CRIVELLI (*c.* 1430–*c.* 1495). The Annunciation (Detail). 1486. Oil on panel. $82\frac{1}{2} \times 58\frac{1}{2}$ in. *London, National Gallery.*

The detail illustrated (actual size) is from the extreme left-hand edge of the painting. The child is looking towards the Virgin, who is kneeling in her chamber, across a courtyard beyond which are seen glimpses of varied and delightful scenes.

Frontispiece. GEORGE KNAPTON (1698–1778). Portrait of Lucy Ebberton. Oil on canvas. $29\frac{1}{2} \times 24\frac{1}{2}$ in. *Dulwich Art Gallery.*

19. EDGAR DEGAS (1834–1917). Woman Washing (Femme à sa toilette). *c.* 1890. Pastel drawing. $28\frac{1}{2} \times 26\frac{1}{2}$ in. *The Lord Clark.*

20. MARY CASSATT (1845–1926). The Morning Toilet. 1886. Oil on canvas. $29\frac{1}{2} \times 24\frac{5}{8}$ in. *Washington, D.C., National Gallery of Art (Chester Dale Collection).*

25. LIVERPOOL PORCELAIN JUG. *c.* 1760. $9\frac{1}{2}$ in. high. *London, Victoria and Albert Museum (Schreiber Collection).*

26. CORNELIS DE VOS (1585–1651). Portrait of a boy. Oil on panel. $48 \times 37\frac{1}{2}$ in. *Antwerp, Musée Mayer van den Bergh.*

35. JOHN ZOFFANY, R.A. (1733–1810). James Sayer fishing. Oil on canvas. 36 × 28 in. *Major Sir Reginald and Lady Macdonald-Buchanan.*

36. CLAUDE MONET (1840–1926). Les Peupliers. 1890. Oil on canvas. 35 × 28½ in. *London, Tate Gallery.*

41. ROELANDT SAVERY (1576–1639). Flowers and Insects. 1611. Oil on panel. 9¼ × 6¾ in. *Private Collection, by courtesy of Messrs. Thomas Agnew & Sons.*

42. JOHN NASH, R.A. (b. 1893). The Moat, Grange Farm, Kimble. *c.* 1922. Oil on canvas. 30 × 20 in. *London, Tate Gallery.*

59. NICHOLAS POCOCK (1741–1821). Nelson's Flagships (Detail). 1807. Oil on panel. 14 × 21 in. *Greenwich, National Maritime Museum.*

The illustration shows half of a commemorative painting of four of the ships in which Nelson served. The *Victory*, Nelson's flagship from 1803 to 1805, is in the foreground. Beyond her is the *Captain*, in which he served in 1796–7.

60. FRENCH TAPESTRY. Le Concert. Fragment of a seventeenth-century tapestry. *Paris, Musée des Gobelins.*

77. JAN JANSZOON TRECK (*c.* 1606–52). Pewter, china and glass. 1649. 30 × 25 in. *London, National Gallery.*

78. WILLIAM STRANG, R.A. (1859–1921). Bank Holiday. 1912. Oil on canvas. 60 × 48 in. *London, Tate Gallery.*

95. GILBERT STUART (1755–1828). The Skater. Oil on canvas. 96½ × 58 in. *Washington, D.C., National Gallery of Art (Mellon Collection).*

96. PIERRE AUGUSTE RENOIR (1841–1919). La Danse. Crayon drawing, 1883. 8$\frac{13}{16}$ × 5$\frac{9}{16}$ in. *The Hon. Michael Astor.*

101. ALFRED WALLIS (1855–1942). Schooner under a Moon. *c.* 1936. Ship's oil-paint on cardboard, mounted on plywood. 11½ × 11½ in. *London, Tate Gallery.*
Alfred Wallis, a Cornish fisherman, was an untaught 'naif' artist.

102. KATSUSHIKA TAITŌ (*fl.* 1816–53). A carp in a pool. Coloured woodcut, Japanese. 14 × 6½ in. *London, Victoria and Albert Museum.*

111. JOHN BRANDARD (1812–63). Lithograph for the cover of *The Express Galop*, composed by Charles d'Albert. *c.* 1850. 11½ × 8½ in. *R. G. L. Rivis, Esq.*
Brandard was one of the two or three most accomplished lithographic artists who designed mid-Victorian music covers.

112. RAOUL DUFY (1877–1953). Jockeys. 1945. Oil on panel. 8¼ × 10⅝ in. *Paris, M. Louis Carré.*

117. SIR PETER LELY (1618–80). A Poet, in the Character of a Shepherd. *c.* 1645. Oil on canvas. 35¼ × 29¼ in. *Dulwich Art Gallery.*

This painting, once at Strawberry Hill, was long supposed to be an idealized portrait of Abraham Cowley, the poet.

118. THOMAS GAINSBOROUGH, R.A. (1727–88). The Honourable Mrs Graham. 1777. Oil on canvas. 92 × 59½ inches. *Edinburgh, National Gallery of Scotland.*

Mrs Graham, who died in 1792 at the age of thirty-five, was perhaps the most beautiful woman to be painted by Gainsborough. This portrait sums up, in one triumphant work of art, the whole Age of Elegance.

135. GEORGE FREDERICK WATTS, R.A. (1817–1904). Choosing: a portrait of Ellen Terry. 1864. Oil on panel. 18½ × 14 in. Exhibited Royal Academy, 1864 and 1951–2. *Formerly in the Collection of the late Kerrison Preston, Esq.*

Watts had married Ellen Terry early in 1864, when she was not quite seventeen.

136. WILLIAM MULREADY, R.A. (1786–1863) The Bathers. 1849. Oil on canvas. 23 × 17½ in. *Dublin, National Gallery of Ireland.*

153. ENGLISH EMBROIDERED PICTURE. Satin, embroidered with silks and seed-pearls. *c.* 1660. 11¾ × 9¼ in. *London, Victoria and Albert Museum.*

154. LIVERPOOL DELFT DISH. *c.* 1760. 11¾ in. diameter. Photograph by courtesy of Messrs. A. F. Allbrook. *Formerly in the collection of the late Mrs. J. Weston.*

171. RICHARD DADD (1817–87). The Fairy Feller's Masterstroke. 1858–64. Oil on canvas. 21 × 15 in. *London, Tate Gallery.*
This is the chief work of an extraordinary painter, who spent the greater part of his life in an asylum. It was painted during his insanity. The subject has been variously interpreted, and appears to embody the 'fire bird' theme. Sir Sacheverell Sitwell summed it up as 'an introduction to the subconscious'.

172. JAMES JOSEPH JACQUES TISSOT (1836–1902). Greenwich. Oil on canvas. 23¼ × 31½ in. *Bodnant, The Lord Aberconway.*
The detail illustrated shows the right-hand side of the painting.

189. PAUL GAUGUIN (1848–1903). Harvesting in Brittany. 1889. Oil on canvas. 36 × 28½ in. *London, Home House Society.*

190. CASPAR NETSCHER (1639–84). The Lace-Maker. 1664. Oil on canvas. 13 × 10½ in. *London, Wallace Collection.*

207. STEFANO DA VERONA (*c.* 1375–*c.* 1440). The Virgin in the Rose Garden. Tempera on panel. *Verona, Castelvecchio.*
The rose garden is the enclosed garden of the Canticle of

Canticles. The Virgin is the Rose of Sharon, and is attended by Saint Catherine of Alexandria, the mystical bride of Christ. The two peacocks symbolize resurrection, and the other birds represent the souls of the faithful.

208. REMBRANDT VAN RIJN (1606–69). Portrait of an Old Man. *c.* 1632. Oil on panel. $22\frac{1}{2}$ × $18\frac{1}{2}$ in. Exhibited in the Loan Exhibition, Slatter Gallery, 1949. *George Schicht, Esq.*

Endpapers: FRENCH TAPESTRY. Noble Pastorale, Danse. Sixteenth century. 88 × 162 in. *Larcade Collection.*

INDEX OF AUTHORS AND ARTISTS

224